devotion.

A RAW TRUTH JOURNAL ON FOLLOWING JESUS

devotion.

A RAW TRUTH JOURNAL ON FOLLOWING JESUS

by Mike Yaconelli

Devotion
Copyright © 2003 by Youth Specialties

Youth Specialties Books, 300 South Pierce Street, El Cajon, CA 92020, are published by
Zondervan, 5300 Patterson Avenue SE, Grand Rapids, MI 49530

Library of Congress Cataloging-in-Publication Data

Yaconelli, Mike.
  [WWJD spiritual challenge journal]
  Devotion : a raw truth journal for following Jesus / by Mike
Yaconelli.
     p. cm.
Originally published: WWJD spiritual challenge journal. Grand Rapids,
Mich. : Zondervan Pub. House, c1999.
Summary: A devotional that presents a New Testament story, a description
of the discipleship trait it presents, a modern-day application, brief
analysis, scriptural references for further reading, and questions to
consider, for each of thirty days.
  ISBN 0-310-25559-7 (pbk.)
  1. Bible. N.T. Gospels--Meditations. 2. Teenagers--Prayer-books and
devotions--English. 3. Church work with youth. [1. Prayer books and
devotions. 2. Christian life.] I. Title.
  BV1485.Y25 2004
  242'.63--dc22

                                                                2003015781

Editorial and art direction by Rick Marschall
Edited by Will Penner
Proofreading by Laura Gross
Cover and interior design by NomadicMedia.net
Design Assistance by Sarah Jongsma
Printed in the United States of America

---

07 08 09 / DC / 11 10 9 8

DEVOTION.

1 ALIENS 2 AUTHORITY 3 BOLDNESS 4 CALLED 5 CLUELE

6 CONFUSION 7 DARING 8 DISCOURAGEMENT 9 DOUBT 10 EMOTION

11 FEAR 12 FRIENDLINESS 13 GENEROSITY 14 HATRED 15 HUMANIT

16 HUNGER 17 IMMATURITY 18 INCAPABLE 19 INDEPENDENCE 20 MATURITY

21 ORDINARY 22 OVERCONFIDENCE 23 PRACTICAL 24 PREPARATION 25 SEEKING

26 SENSITIVITY 27 SERVANT-LIKE 28 SHREWDNESS 29 STRENGTH 30 WEAKNESS

devotion.

A RAW TRUTH JOURNAL ON FOLLOWING JESUS

aliens

Aliens are foreigners, strangers in a strange land. Aliens don't speak the native language, don't follow the customs and traditions, and don't fit in. Aliens are typically uncomfortable, awkward, and unsure of themselves in their new foreign homes.

¶ Disciples are aliens in this world. Many of the values found within our culture are foreign to disciples. Disciples don't naturally fit into a society that's largely out of touch with God. They're uncomfortable-looking, and they feel out of place in the everyday world. Disciples of Christ find themselves continually at odds with the culture, because they have different values, different priorities, and a different language. Disciples feel odd and estranged in contemporary culture—and that's just how they ought to feel.

Life Hint:
Fitting in is not always a good thing.

L

1 Peter 2:9-12
You say "different" like it's a bad thing?

But you are a chosen people, a royal priesthood, a holy nation, a people belonging to God, that you may declare the praises of him who called you out of darkness into his wonderful light. Once you were not a people, but now you are the people of God; once you had not received mercy, but now you have received mercy. Dear friends, I urge you, as aliens and strangers in the world, to abstain from sinful desires, which war against your soul. Live such good lives among the pagans that, though they accuse you of doing wrong, they may see your good deeds and glorify God on the day he visits us.

FACT FOR THE DAY
ROBERT HEINLEIN WROTE THE SCIENCE FICTION BOOK *STRANGER IN A STRANGE LAND* IN 1961. IT'S THE STORY OF AN ALIEN WHO COMES TO EARTH AND CAN'T FIT IN, SO HE ESTABLISHES A NEW RELIGION.

TODAY'S TOP 10
MAKE A LIST OF THE TOP TEN THINGS THAT MAKE YOU DIFFERENT FROM EVERYONE ELSE.

JOURNAL ENTRY:
THE MORE I TRY TO BE LIKE EVERYONE ELSE THE MORE I BUILD WALLS AROUND MYSELF. I NEED TO TEAR DOWN THE WALLS. I NEED TO CELEBRATE WHO I AM. I TAKE TODAY AND I WILL…

All that makes you different and unique in this world is a gift from God. Following the One who said to be different is a way to say thank you. May you celebrate that which others condemn in you. God does.

Someone Just Like You

Diane (some people called her "Lady Di" because she looked just like the late Princess of Wales) found herself at the center of the conversation. The slumber party had been going strong since last night, and now, at three in the morning, the talk was getting serious. ¶ "Come on, Diane, what do you mean you've never looked at a Victoria's Secret catalog? It's more than the underwear, which, frankly, I can't believe you don't care about. It's the models. They look so good. I want to know their secret; don't you?" ¶ "Not really," Di said. "That's why I don't go out with guys right now. I'm too young, too easily influenced by guys. I could easily be obsessed with how I look. And I know this sounds stupid, but my faith really matters to me. Thinking about guys and about my body and my clothes and my makeup all the time doesn't make a lot of sense when I could be learning more about God." ¶ "Get real, Di. The only reason you're saying that is because you already have a body worth dying for and looks to go with it. Every guy in class wants to go out with you. I mean, come on, you want to learn more about God? That's psycho. What's wrong with you?" ¶ Diane sat up, not sure if it was anger or hurt feelings that she felt inside. ¶ "Hey, I know, I know. Girls are considered crazy if they don't sit around drooling over guys and trying to turn them on by wearing tight skirts and miracle bras. Frankly, I don't like being pretty because it keeps people from trying to get to know me. I think it's sick to turn on guys just so I can feel good. Besides, I don't want some horny guy who just likes my body. Call me weird if you want, but I'm totally happy to have no guys in my life right now." ¶ The conversation ended awkwardly, and Diane eventually fell asleep. Later on that night something woke her up. She would rather not have heard the whispered conversation that was going on. ¶ "...but she doesn't make sense. She's full of crap and you know it. Either Diane's lying or she's a lesbian." "I wouldn't be surprised if she was a lesbian." "She's just plain weird. All this talk about God is a bunch of baloney." ¶ Diane pretended to turn over in her sleep so no one could see her crying.

DE

party, what would you say to her?

IN THE STORY

If you were Diane's best friend and she came to you with what happened at the

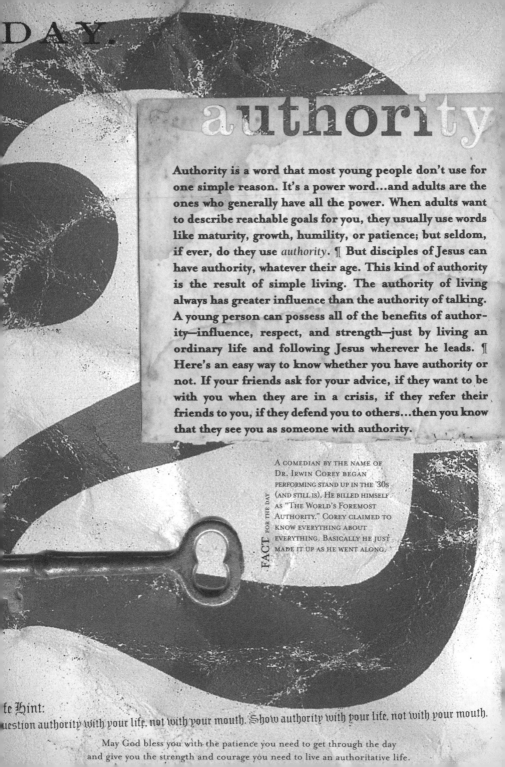

authority

Authority is a word that most young people don't use for one simple reason. It's a power word...and adults are the ones who generally have all the power. When adults want to describe reachable goals for you, they usually use words like maturity, growth, humility, or patience; but seldom, if ever, do they use *authority*. ¶ But disciples of Jesus can have authority, whatever their age. This kind of authority is the result of simple living. The authority of living always has greater influence than the authority of talking. A young person can possess all of the benefits of authority—influence, respect, and strength—just by living an ordinary life and following Jesus wherever he leads. ¶ Here's an easy way to know whether you have authority or not. If your friends ask for your advice, if they want to be with you when they are in a crisis, if they refer their friends to you, if they defend you to others...then you know that they see you as someone with authority.

FACT FOR THE DAY

A COMEDIAN BY THE NAME OF DR. IRWIN COREY BEGAN PERFORMING STAND UP IN THE '30S (AND STILL IS). HE BILLED HIMSELF AS "THE WORLD'S FOREMOST AUTHORITY." COREY CLAIMED TO KNOW EVERYTHING ABOUT EVERYTHING. BASICALLY HE JUST MADE IT UP AS HE WENT ALONG.

fe Hint:
uestion authority with your life, not with your mouth. Show authority with your life, not with your mouth.

May God bless you with the patience you need to get through the day
and give you the strength and courage you need to live an authoritative life.

Someone Just Like You

Rick is one of those very bright people other kids tolerate but don't like to hang out with. Rick knows all his "friends" at church put up with him because they need him now and then to fix their computers or bail them out at test time or to explain the latest calculus assignment. For some reason, Rick never worries much about his nerd status. He has a lot of self-confidence and has no huge need to be cool. A lot of his confidence comes from his faith in Jesus.

¶ Rick has always lived on the outside of life. His divorced parents have little time for him. He lives with his grandmother, who barely copes with her own arthritis and other old-age ailments. His brother and two sisters have long since gone their own ways—ways that are cluttered with drugs, alcohol, and repeated trouble. When Rick heard about Jesus and understood that Jesus not only died for him but also wanted him as a disciple, it was all Rick needed to hear. Not being wanted by anyone else only made Jesus' "wanting" of Rick more powerful in his life. When Gina—the very popular and very sexy Gina—realized she was pregnant, it was Rick she asked for help and advice. When Mark—the very good-looking and very popular Mark—realized he was the father but didn't want to get married right away, he called Rick as well. Rick was surprised and, deep down inside himself, rather pleased. He realized that, although his faith in Jesus Christ hadn't gotten rid of his nerdiness, it had given him authority.

IN THE STORY Is there a "Rick" in your church? Are you the "Rick"? What would you say if the popular pregnant girl (or the father) came to you?

Today's TOP 10

MAKE A LIST OF THE TOP TEN THINGS YOU DO EVERY DAY THAT ARE YOUR CHOICE TO DO.

JOURNAL ENTRY:

I CAN CHOOSE THE KIND OF LIFE I LIVE. I CAN CHOOSE WHAT I BELIEVE. I CAN CHOOSE TO CONTROL MYSELF OR NOT. I HAVE AUTHORITY OVER MY DECISIONS. I CAN CHOOSE TO BE. . . .

Mark 2:23-28
Religion gets in the way of faith.

One Sabbath Jesus was going through the grainfields, and as his disciples walked along, they began to pick some heads of grain. The Pharisees said to him, "Look, why are they doing what is unlawful on the Sabbath?" He answered, "Have you never read what David did when he and his companions were hungry and in need? In the days of Abiathar the high priest, he entered the house of God and ate the consecrated bread, which is lawful only for priests to eat. And he also gave some to his companions." Then he said to them, "The Sabbath was made for man, not man for the Sabbath. So the Son of Man is Lord even of the Sabbath."

three.

Boldness doesn't mean rude, obnoxious, loud, or disrespectful. Being bold is being firm, sure, confident, fearless, daring, strong, resilient, and not easily intimidated. It means you're willing to go where you've never been, willing to try what you've never tried, and willing to trust what you've never trusted. Boldness is quiet, not noisy. Jesus' boldness in front of Pilate was his silence...and Pilate was blown away by it. Being bold is remaining firm when everyone around you yells at you to give in. Boldness is telling people what you believe even when your beliefs earn you ridicule. Boldness is a secret strength that others respect even when they act like they don't.

When you decide to follow God instead of following your friends, you are being bold. When you say no to your girlfriend or boyfriend because you are saying yes to God, you're being bold. Boldness isn't something you're born with; you either choose it or you don't.

TODAY'S **TOP** 10

MAKE A LIST OF THE TOP TEN "BOLDEST" PEOPLE YOU KNOW. (YOU CAN INCLUDE YOURSELF IF YOU WANT TO.)

JOURNAL ENTRY:

START HERE. OKAY, SO IF GOING DOWN THIS PATH WITH JESUS COULD GET ME HURT AND GET ME IN TROUBLE, WHY DO IT? I'M GOING TO DO IT BECAUSE...

Matthew 10:34-39

Following Jesus is not a part-time job.

"Do not suppose that I have come to bring peace to the earth. I did not come to bring peace, but a sword. For I have come to turn 'a man against his father, a daughter against her mother, a daughter-in-law against her mother-in-law—a man's enemies will be the members of his own household.' Anyone who loves his father or mother more than me is not worthy of me; anyone who loves his son or daughter more than me is not worthy of me; and anyone who does not take his cross and follow me is not worthy of me. Whoever finds his life will lose it, and whoever loses his life for my sake will find it."

FACT FOR THE DAY
ACCORDING TO THE BOLD
SECTION OF THE PROCTOR
AND GAMBLE WEBSITE, FRESH
BLOODSTAINS COME OUT BETTER
IF THEY ARE IMMEDIATELY
SOAKED IN COLD WATER.*

*SOURCE: WWW.PG.COM/MAIN.JHTML

May you be bold in your beliefs and take courage, even if you're put down for what you believe in the examples of Daniel, David, and Noah. May you be bold in heart, word, and deed.

render thanks. How

Someone Just Like You

FROM THE STORY Put yourself in LeAnne's mother's shoes...what would be the next thing you'd say to her?

LeAnne was excited. What a surprise this would be for her mom and dad! While finishing her senior year at high school she'd written to Youth With a Mission and been accepted for discipleship training on the Mercy Ship, docked then in South Africa. She would spend the summer raising the $6,000 needed to fly to South Africa in September. Yes, she'd have to delay college for a few months, but YWAM and South Africa seemed like where God wanted LeAnne. Of course her parents would support her decision. ¶ She couldn't have been more wrong. Her parents were hurt because she had told them earlier about her plans. They were outraged that she was delaying going college "after all they had done." Going to a nation with a recent history of politi instability and racial conflict, they argued, was just plain dangerous. LeAnne's mo and dad made it very clear: South Africa was simply out of the question. Not an optic School was the only option. And frankly, they added, they had serious questio about the church LeAnne was attending and any youth program that would encoura such insanity. ¶ Never in her 18 years had LeAnne felt so distant from her paren They had always been supportive of everything she'd done. They loved her you group, loved her church. She was shocked, surprised, and shaken—and yet, she strangely calm inside. She heard herself saying, "I'm sorry you feel the way you Mom and Dad. I know you love me, and I love you. I appreciate everything you h done for me...and I'm going to South Africa."

Life Hint: Bold hurts (sometimes).

called

Called is a strange word. You don't hear it much. You hear career; you hear job; you hear interest. People usually ask you about what you do, not what your calling is. But a calling is more than a job or career or something you do. A calling has to do with who you are. When God said to Jeremiah, "Before I formed you in the womb I knew you," he was talking about a calling (Jeremiah 1:5). A calling has to do with how we're made (read Psalm 139 for more on that). A calling is the place where your gifts, abilities, desires, and feelings of worth all meet. When you follow your calling, you feel at home, at peace—you feel as though you're where you're meant to be. ¶ A calling is always accompanied by passion. When you discover your calling, you'll be filled with joy, gratitude, and often tears. Your calling is the brand of God on your soul, the source of energy, renewal, and life. Disciples are more than people who believe in Jesus—they're people who follow him by listening to how they're made. A bunch of rugged fishermen with calloused hands that stunk of fish discovered that they were made for more than netting fish. They were made to fish for men and women.

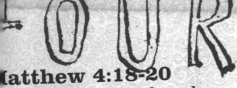

Matthew 4:18-20

Jesus didn't mince words, and the disciples didn't mince action.

As Jesus was walking beside the Sea of Galilee, he saw two brothers, Simon called Peter and his brother Andrew. They were casting a net into the lake, for they were fishermen. "Come, follow me," Jesus said, "and I will make you fishers of men." At once they left their nets and followed him.

TODAY'S **TOP 10**
MAKE A LIST OF THE TOP TEN THINGS YOU DO, NOT BECAUSE YOU ENJOY DOING THEM, BUT BECAUSE IT JUST "FEELS RIGHT" WHEN YOU DO THEM. (THESE CAN BE AS SIMPLE AS BAKING A CAKE OR AS COMPLEX AS GOING ON A DIFFICULT MISSION TRIP.)

JOURNAL ENTRY:

IMAGINE YOU HAVE A DREAM AND JESUS COMES AND SITS WITH YOU AT A DINER AND SAYS, "I'VE BEEN TAKING A LOOK AT YOUR LIFE, AND I'M REALLY PLEASED SO FAR. BASED ON THE GIFTS I'VE GIVEN YOU AND WHAT I NEED DONE IN THE WORLD, I THINK I'D LIKE YOU TO…"

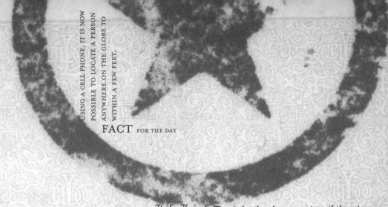

USING A CELL PHONE, IT IS NOW POSSIBLE TO LOCATE A PERSON ANYWHERE ON THE GLOBE TO WITHIN A FEW FEET.

FACT FOR THE DAY

Life Hint: Don't bother hammering if there's no na

May God give you the ears to listen for his voice, and may you hear and understand it—
and have the courage to act.

"What are you going to major in?" keeps coming up with more intensity "Look, Curt," his dad said firmly, "You can't keep floundering aroun trying to figure out what you're going to do with your life." ¶ "I know Dad. We've gone over the same ground all summer long. I just don know what I want to do. All I know is that I want to do something fo God, and I think that something is writing." ¶ "Look, Curt, writin for God is fine. But you have to get your head out of the clouds and int the real world. I can make it easy for you to join my law firm. You ca control the amount of hours you want to work in the practice, and th rest of the time you can write." ¶ "Thanks, Dad. I mean, it all sound sensible and reasonable, but sometimes God doesn't work sensibly an reasonably. Anyway, I don't need to decide right now. I don't have m head in the clouds. I'm just listening to my soul, to the way I'm made You're good with words, Mom is an English teacher, and I'm only wantin to be what both of you made me to be—what God made me to be." ¶ "Your mother and I did not make you a bum and neither did God and that's what will happen to you if you keep being so fanatical." ¶ "I am not a fanatic, Dad. I'm a Christian. I'm trying to follow Chris just like you and Mom. At least that's why I thought you made sure I wer to church. I can't believe you think I'm a fanatic." ¶ "We went to churc because we thought a little religion might provide a healthy environmen for our family. We didn't think you'd go crazy." ¶ "It's not crazy to follow the way you're made, and it's not fanatical. I didn't 'get religion,' Dad. I found a way to honor the way you and Mom have raised me." ¶ "If that's the way you honor your father and mother, then you'd better go back and read your Bible. You honor us by obeying us, and right now you're disobeying us."

Someone Just Like You

Imagine you are Curt's youth minister and he's asked you to go with him to talk to his parents. What's your opening line?

clue

5

Clueless means oblivious, which is a fancy word for unaware, unsuspecting, or caught by surprise. When you're clueless, you have no idea of what's going on. You don't understand what you're seeing or hearing. You know, like duh. ¶ Most people assume that the longer you know God, the more you know about God. So maybe it's more accurate to say that the longer you know God, the less clueless you are, the less surprised you are by him. But it's also accurate to say the more you know about God, the more you realize how little you really know about him. ¶ What does all this mean? It means that being a disciple is being clueless. As you spend more time with Jesus, you become less clueless about his ways and more aware of how mysterious he really is. Think about how exciting it is to be a disciple. Friendship with Jesus is a continuous growing process in which God becomes both more familiar and more mysterious at the same time.

FACT FOR THE DAY
THE HASBRO BOARD GAME
CLUE WAS CREATED IN 1963. IN
THE BRITISH VERSION, VICTIM
MR. BODDY IS REFERRED TO AS
DR. BLACK, AND SUSPECT MR.
GREEN IS A MINISTER.

*SOURCE: WWW.MYSTERY-GAMES.COM/LEONDAVINANJ.HTML

TODAY'S TOP 10
MAKE A LIST OF THE TOP TEN THINGS
YOU KNOW FOR SURE ABOUT GOD.

JOURNAL ENTRY:

GOD MAY NOT HAVE ALWAYS GIVEN ME
EVERYTHING I WANT, BUT I'M SURE
THAT GOD IS REAL BECAUSE...

May God give you the understanding that you don't need to understand him in order to love him.

While Jesus was in Bethany in the home of a man known as Simon the Leper, a woman came to him with an alabaster jar of very expensive perfume, which she poured on his head as he was reclining at the table. When the disciples saw this, they were indignant. "Why this waste?" they asked. "This perfume could have been sold at a high price and the money given to the poor."

Aware of this, Jesus said to them "Why are you bothering this woman? She has done a beautiful thing to me. The poor you will always have with you, but you will not always have me. When she poured this perfume on my body, she did it to prepare me for burial. I tell you the truth, wherever this gospel is preached throughout the world, what she has done will also be told, in memory of her."

Carver had been invited to the youth group by the youth pastor. Carver was active in a church downtown, an urban church, 99% black, populated almost exclusively by people who lived in the south part of town. Southside was the most dangerous section of the city, the turf of a number of gangs. Not a day went by that Southside wasn't mentioned in the paper for a drive-by shooting, a murder, or some other crime. So Carver was something of a celebrity in First Church's all-white suburban church. Carver spoke about how difficult it was to live where he did when every night brought nonstop gunfire. The kids of First Church were spellbound and had many questions¶ "Must be difficult to grow up not knowing who your dad is," someone blurted out. ¶ Carver responded graciously, "Yeah, but I know who my mom is. She's an amazing person— tough, hard working, and demanding—but she sure does love me and support everything I do. I don't think many of you have a relationship with your mom like I do with mine."¶ "But isn't it scary living so close to gunfire every night?" ¶ "Yes it is, but it's really helped me get closer to God. Not because I ask him to protect me, but more because I'm conscious of his presence with me. That's something I experience every day. I don't think many people experience that closeness more than once or twice in their lives." ¶ "Yeah, but wouldn't you rather live in a peaceful area, away from all the violence and noise?"   ¶ "No, I would much rather live in a place like mine," Carver shot back sarcastically. "Are you kidding? Of course I'd rather live where it's safe. But I can't. I won't leave my mom and we can't afford to live somewhere else. So I've got to live where I live. But it isn't like the movies, you know. We're all family in our neighborhood, and we look out for each other. Look, I don't want to be mean or anything, but it's tough living where I do and it's tough being black in a white society. But this Jesus thing is for real. He's been there for me, you know? What I mean is, he's been there for me in ways I can't describe. He ain't got me out of the city. He ain't made my mom's life any easier. He ain't brought my dad back. But I know he's real, 'cause he's been there for me! I only wish I could tell you what that means to me, but I can't."

IN THE STORY How would you encourage Carver to express himself?

Confusion means you're mixed up, unclear. In other words, you don't get it. Confusion happens all the time. We don't understand what our parents mean; we don't understand the pastor's sermon; we don't understand a Bible verse; we don't understand what we're supposed to do next. Being confused is actually not so bad, because it usually results in being unconfused. Often when you're confused you're on the brink of a new insight or new awareness. ¶ Of course, when you're in the midst of confusion, you feel kind of stupid. You doubt yourself. You wonder whether you messed up or weren't listening to something important. Most of the time, though, confusion comes because we don't have all the pieces to the puzzle in front of us. So we just have to wait for more puzzle pieces. Meanwhile, don't apologize for being confused. Admit your confusion, learn from it, and start growing.

Luke 22:14-23

You are what you eat.

When the hour came, Jesus and his apostles reclined at the table. And he said to them, "I have eagerly desired to eat this Passover with you before I suffer. For I tell you, I will not eat it again until it finds fulfillment in the kingdom of God."

After taking the cup, he gave thanks and said, "Take this and divide it among you. For I tell you I will not drink again of the fruit of the vine until the kingdom of God comes." And he took bread, gave thanks and broke it, and gave it to them, saying, "This is my body given for you; do this in remembrance of me."

In the same way, after the supper he took the cup, saying, "This cup is the new covenant in my blood, which is poured out for you. But the hand of him who is going to betray me is with mine on the table. The Son of Man will go as it has been decreed, but woe to that man who betrays him." They began to question among themselves which of them it might be who would do this.

May God help you be satisfied with your not-knowing.

Someone Just Like You

Trina thought she had prayer figured out. She had just finished a six-week study on the topic in her youth group. She learned that prayer isn't just asking for stuff from God; it's much more than that. It involves listening to God, opening up to him, talking with him. In other words, prayer is conversation, communion, and connecting with God at a deep level. For years Trina had seen prayer as a way to get God to do what she wanted rather than a way for God to get what he wanted from her. ¶ Trina had prayed for years that her dad and mom wouldn't get a divorce. Unfortunately, last year they did. Trina was now able to see that the divorce wasn't God's fault. She felt better about God than she had in years—until a few minutes ago, that is. ¶ Jennifer had just called to share her excitement. "Trina, you'll never believe what's happened! You know how my mom has cancer and everyone in the church has been praying for her? Well, she went to the doctor today to get the results of her test, and the cancer is gone! The doctors can't understand what happened, but we know. God answered our prayers!"

¶ Instead of being excited for Jennifer, Trina was angry. God answered her prayer? Trina asked herself. Why didn't he answer my prayer? Why did I have to lose my family? What, I'm not a good enough Christian? I didn't pray enough? I didn't pray right? Is this prayer thing some cruel joke that I just don't get?

Life Hint: "Jesus loves me, this I know"...and that's all you need to

Today's TOP 10

MAKE A LIST OF THE TOP TEN THINGS THAT CONFUSE THE HECK OUT OF YOU.

FACT FOR THE DAY

CURRENTLY ONE OF THE LARGEST JIGSAW PUZZLES IN THE WORLD IS CREATED BY THE CLEMENTONI COMPANY OF ITALY. IT DEPICTS THE ANGEL GABRIEL APPEARING TO THE VIRGIN MARY. IT MEASURES MORE THAN 115 INCHES ACROSS AND HAS MORE THAN 13,000 PIECES.*

JOURNAL ENTRY:

I THINK THE REASON I HAVE TROUBLE WITH JUST BEING IN THE PRESENCE OF GOD RATHER THAN KNOWING EVERY-THING ABOUT THE PRESENCE IS...

*SOURCE: WWW.MYSTERY-GAMES.COM/LEONDAVINANJ.HTML

TE DARING

Daring is one characteristic of a disciple people don't talk about very much. It sounds so adventurous...and dangerous. Daring people are kind of crazy, and daring disciples are kind of crazy for God. Being daring for God means being willing to go wherever Jesus wants to take us. Jesus wants us to touch people others say are untouchable? Okay. Jesus says we need to go into the temple and shake up the business leaders and religious dudes? Okay, I guess so. Jesus says it looks like things could get real dangerous? No problem. Daring is the quality in disciples that actually makes other people afraid of them. Daring disciples are truly different, and when you are different in this culture, you make others nervous.

Jesus lets everyone know exactly whom they're dealing with Luke 5:17-26

One day as he was teaching, Pharisees and teachers of the law, who had come from every village of Galilee and from Judea and Jerusalem, were sitting there. And the power of the Lord was present for him to heal the sick. Some men came carrying a paralytic on a mat and tried to take him into the house to lay him before Jesus. When they could not find a way to do this because of the crowd, they went up on the roof and lowered him on his mat through the tiles into the middle of the crowd, right in front of Jesus. When Jesus saw their faith, he said, "Friend, your sins are forgiven."

The Pharisees and the teachers of the law began thinking to themselves, "Who is this fellow who speaks blasphemy? Who can forgive sins but God alone?"

Jesus knew what they were thinking and asked, "Why are you thinking these things in your hearts? Which is easier: to say, 'Your sins are forgiven,' or to say, 'Get up and walk'? But that you may know that the Son of Man has authority on earth to forgive sins...." He said to the paralyzed man, "I tell you, get up, take your mat and go home." Immediately he stood up in front of them, took what he had been lying on and went home praising God.

Everyone was amazed and gave praise to God. They were filled with awe and said, "We have seen remarkable things today."

Someone Just Like You

My name is Jenine. Ariane, my best friend, and I will be graduating in two weeks. Ever since Ariane and I were in the seventh grade, we've had our lives planned. Neither one of us comes from a family with lots of money. Both of us have to work during the summer to help with school costs. Luckily, both Ariane and I are good students—we received partial scholarships to Florida State University. ¶ But just when I thought everything was looking great for this summer, Ariane flipped out. Out of nowhere she announced she's not getting a job. Instead, she's working with her church youth group and going with them on a mission trip to Haiti. It's crazy! Now the plans we've made together for five years are ruined. Instead of going to FSU, where she has a scholarship, she's going to stay home and attend a local junior college part-time without a scholarship. ¶ We've been good friends for a long time. I knew she went to church with her mom, but I didn't think she was serious about it. I mean, she's being so stupid! She's betraying our friendship, she's wasting a scholarship, and she's delaying her graduation from college (if she ever graduates) to help with a bunch of silly junior high kids at her church. Besides, Haiti is dangerous. ¶ I've pleaded with Ariane to rethink what she's doing, but she won't listen. All of our friends have tried to talk to her. You know what she says? "Hey, you guys, I'm tired of our lives. All we do is go to movies, talk about boys, go out with boys, talk about more boys, try to look sexy, talk about sex, and go to school when we don't even know what we want to do. I'm bored with all that. I want to take some risks this summer. I want to help some kids. I want to help the poor. I'm not saying you guys are doing the wrong thing, but my faith is actually starting to sound exciting to me." ¶ Can you believe Ariane? Her religion is exciting? I think she's lost it. I really do. She sounds like one of those Waco people to me. I'm glad I found this out about her now.

May God give you the courage to make all those around you nervous.

What would you say to Jenine?

FACT for the day

In the 1970s a daredevil named Evil Knievel made history by jumping over fountains, cars, buses, and various other things with a motorcycle. He is in The Guinness World Records book for most broken bones (35) and is responsible for the phrase "Kids, don't try this at home."*

*Source:
www.biography.com

Today's **TOP 10**
MAKE A LIST OF THE TOP TEN THINGS YOU DO THAT SCARE OTHERS.

JOURNAL Entry:
I SING HYMNS QUIETLY BECAUSE I DON'T WANT PEOPLE TO LOOK AT ME. I DON'T SPEAK UP IN BIBLE STUDY CAUSE I'M NOT SMART ENOUGH. THAT ALL ENDS NOW; FROM NOW ON...

IN THE STORY
Let's say you've known Jenine for years but you've never met Ariane.

Discouragement isn't a bad thing; it's a normal thing. Feeling discouraged is the shadow side of growing up. When hormones continually attack your body (as in the case of most teenagers), there are days when you just wake up feeling bad. The secret is to wait those kinds of days out, knowing things will get better. Then there are those days when feeling bad is justified. The two disciples in the story felt bad because life looked hopeless. Their faith in shambles, they had a million questions with no answers. So of course they felt bad. Though Jesus got a little frustrated with them, he also reminded the men of what they'd forgotten. Then he had communion with them! Discouragement and discipleship go together. Because disciples believe intensely, they crash and burn intensely. Discouragement is part of being a disciple.

Life Hint:
A light burns all the brighter in the midst of darkness.

Today's TOP 10
MAKE A LIST OF THE TOP TEN THINGS ABOUT LIFE THAT MAKE YOU WANT TO STAY IN BED.

JOURNAL Entry:
WHEN I LOOK BACK ON THE WORST THING THAT EVER HAPPENED TO ME I AMAZED TO SEE THAT…

May you feel the presence of Jesus beside you on your worst (and your best) days. May God grant you the patience to hold on until the dawn.

FACT FOR THE DAY
THE PHRASE "BAD HAIR DAY" CAME INTO PLAY AFTER THE MOVIE VERSION OF *Buffy the Vampire Slayer*. BUFFY (KRISTY SWANSON) SAID IT TO A ONE-ARMED VAMPIRE PLAYED BY PAUL RUBENS. THE LINE IS: "I'M FINE, BUT YOU'RE OBVIOUSLY HAVING A BAD HAIR DAY."*

*SOURCE: HTTP://PHRASES.SHU.AC.UK/INDEX.HTML

IN THE STORY

What would this girl say after spending the evening with your church youth group?

What advice would you give to her?

Every time I go to youth group I get the same types of comments: Hey, what's wrong with you? Why so blue? Lighten up! Feeling all right? Okay, I'll admit I'm moody. I feel sad a lot of the time. To be honest, the only time I feel absolutely exhilarated is when I'm dancing. I love any kind of dancing, really—hip hop, jazz, ballet…it doesn't matter, as long as it's dance. Something happens to me when I dance. I know it sounds weird; but I feel close to God, I feel great about life, and I feel like I'm on top of the world. ¶ Trouble is, when I go to our weekly Bible study on campus, everyone there thinks I'm not a very good Christian. They're always telling me to cheer up, to notify my face about how I should be feeling since I know Jesus. I'm a Christian, and I'm trying to be a good one; but I'm not a very "up" person. Sometimes I wonder if Christianity is just for the I'm-always-happy people…or can someone like me be a follower of Christ?

When you're up or when you're down…
Jesus is there.

Now that same day two of them were going to a village called Emmaus, about seven miles from Jerusalem. They were talking with each other about everything that had happened. As they talked and discussed these things with each other, Jesus himself came up and walked along with them; but they were kept from recognizing him. He asked them, "What are you discussing together as you walk along?" They stood still, their faces downcast. One of them, named Cleopas, asked him, "Are you only a visitor to Jerusalem and do not know the things that have happened there in these days?"

"What things?" he asked.

"About Jesus of Nazareth," they replied. "He was a prophet, powerful in word and deed before God and all the people. The chief priests and our rulers handed him over to be sentenced to death, and they crucified him; but we had hoped that he was the one who was going to redeem Israel. And what is more, it is the third day since all this took place. In addition, some of our women amazed us. They went to the tomb early this morning but didn't find his body. They came and told us that they had seen a vision of angels, who said he was alive. Then some of our companions went to the tomb and found it just as the women had said, but him they did not see."

He said to them, "How foolish you are, and how slow of heart to believe all that the prophets have spoken! Did not the Christ have to suffer these things and then enter his glory?" And beginning with Moses and all the Prophets, he explained to them what was said in all the Scriptures concerning himself.

John 20:24-29
Jesus has Thomas do the hokey pokey.

Now Thomas (called Didymus), one of the Twelve, was not with the disciples when Jesus came. So the other disciples told him, "We have seen the Lord!"

But he said to them, "Unless I see the nail marks in his hands and put my finger where the nails were, and put my hand into his side, I will not believe it."

doubt

A week later his disciples were in the house again, and Thomas was with them. Though the doors were locked, Jesus came and stood among them and said, "Peace be with you!" Then he said to Thomas, "Put your finger here; see my hands. Reach out your hand and put it into my side. Stop doubting and believe." Thomas said to him, "My Lord and my God!"

Then Jesus told him, "Because you have seen me, you have believed; blessed are those who have not seen and yet have believed."

TODAY'S TOP 10

MAKE A LIST OF THE TOP TEN COMMON-LY ACCEPTED IDEAS THAT MAKE YOU GO, "HMMMM..." (ASSUMPTIONS THAT OTHERS HAVE BUT THAT YOU DON'T THINK ARE TRUE.)

Doubt stems from questions that keep us from believing. Generally you have to be very brave to be a doubter, because believers generally don't like doubters. There are all kinds of doubt, of course. There are lazy doubters who simply use their questions to avoid the responsibility of belief. There are cynical doubters who question everything just because they like to shake everyone else's beliefs. We doubt when we don't know, we doubt when we're afraid to know, and we doubt when we don't want to know. But most of the time disciples doubt because they are confused or lost.

¶ Thomas knew the cost of being a disciple and was willing to die for it (John 11:16); however, he was not willing to have a secondhand faith. He doubted whether the disciples had seen Jesus. He wanted to touch the resurrected Jesus himself as proof. Jesus' response to Thomas is very important for disciples to understand. Instead of rejecting Thomas and banishing him from the disciples, Jesus honored his doubts and showed up! Disciples doubt from time to time, and Jesus honors our doubts. In effect, Jesus says, "I wish you didn't doubt, but I love you because your faith is so important that you are brave enough to ask the questions of your soul."

Someone Just Like You

Juanita's parents are not Christians. They refuse to attend church with their daughter or talk about God, period. Juanita had become a Christian about a year ago. Before she gave her life to God, her grades were barely above Cs, her relationship with her parents was terrible, and she was hanging around drug dealers and users. Juanita was very close to disaster in her life. ¶ But everything is different now. Juanita's grades are much better, she has a new group of friends—mostly from the youth group—and she stays home to help her parents around the house, because both of them work. Juanita figured her parents had to be pleased with the changes in her life, but they'd never said a word. After a while, Juanita would say things like, "Mom and Dad, aren't you glad I know God? Don't you notice the difference in my life?" ¶ "We're not going to talk to you about God, Juanita," they replied, "so forget it. You are the same Juanita we've known all your life." ¶ Juanita was very discouraged. She'd been praying for her parents for a year now, with no change. Every day she waited to see if God was going to do something with her parents. Every day she became more discouraged. She was beginning to doubt that Christianity was for real. ¶ Sunday was Juanita's birthday. She woke up early because her parents wanted to celebrate before she went to church. They had plans for the rest of the day, so they agreed on an early breakfast celebration. Breakfast was fun, with 18 sausage candles on a pancake cake. ¶ When it came time for Juanita's gift, there was no package, just a small envelope. Inside was a simple two-page handwritten letter from her father. Here is what it said:

Dear Juanita,

A long time ago my brother committed suicide. When my parents went to the church to ask for a funeral, they were told they didn't give enough money. Besides, they were told, suicide was a sin. My parents never went back to church, and neither did I. I hated God and religion. About a year ago your mother and I were very worried about you. We were at the end of our rope when suddenly you just changed. When you told us Jesus was the reason, I couldn't handle it. All the memories came back, and I was very angry and bitter. But over the last few months you have been so different that I realized whatever had happened had to be real. I knew you wanted us to say something, but I just couldn't. I had a lot of anger. I went to counseling and I'm starting to do better. So, after a lot of thinking and talking, your mother and I have decided to give you a birthday present I hope you want. We have decided to start going to church with you starting this morning. I'm not promising that your mother and I are going to be instant saints, but if we can be anything like you, we'll be happy.

Love,
Dad

Juanita's eyes filled with tears. Quietly, she thought, *Oh, God, I am so sorry I doubted you. This is going to be a great birthday.*

IN THE STORY Write a note from Juanita to her father.

JOURNAL ENTRY:
I REALLY WANT TO BELIEVE, BUT I CAN'T SEEM TO JUMP FULL FORCE INTO THE BELIEVER'S POOL. I THINK IT'S OKAY IF I TEST THE WATERS FIRST; MAYBE I CAN START BY…

FACT FOR THE DAY

ALTHOUGH A LOT OF THE ART DEPICTS THOMAS GENTLY TOUCHING THE HOLES IN JESUS' HAND, THE ORIGINAL GREEK TRANSLATION OF THE PHRASE LITERALLY MEANT JESUS WAS ASKING THOMAS TO "SHOVE" OR "JAM" HIS FINGER THROUGH THE HOLE.

Emotional means passionate, excitable, and intense. It can also mean fickle, unstable, temperamental, and unpredictable. When people are so in touch with their emotions that they listen to their feelings instead of their reason, they can sometimes end up in trouble. But reason can get us into trouble, too. Reason and logic can keep us from experiencing the highs and lows of life that should be experienced by everyone, especially a follower of Jesus. ¶ On the other hand, emotions can be shallow and manipulative. Emotional people often use their emotions instead of experiencing and listening to those emotions. A girl may cry when her boyfriend breaks up with her because she is genuinely sad, or she may cry because she hopes her tears will cause her boyfriend to decide to stay in the relationship. An angry guy may find a way to resolve his anger, or he may decide to act on it. He may use his anger to right a wrong, or he may give into the anger and create another wrong. Strong emotions can give us the strength to persevere or become the basis of giving up. Emotional people are usually up and down a lot—but they also hug a lot, too.

Matthew 17:1-9
Can you ride a roller coaster without screaming?

After six days Jesus took with him Peter, James and John the brother of James, and led them up a high mountain by themselves. There he was transfigured before them. His face shone like the sun, and his clothes became as white as the light. Just then there appeared before them Moses and Elijah, talking with Jesus.

Peter said to Jesus, "Lord, it is good for us to be here. If you wish, I will put up three shelters—one for you, one for Moses and one for Elijah."

While he was still speaking, a bright cloud enveloped them, and a voice from the cloud said, "This is my Son, whom I love; with him I am well pleased. Listen to him!" When the disciples heard this, they fell facedown to the ground, terrified. But Jesus came and touched them. "Get up," he said. "Don't be afraid." When they looked up, they saw no one except Jesus.

As they were coming down the mountain, Jesus instructed them, "Don't tell anyone what you have seen, until the Son of Man has been raised from the dead."

FACT FOR THE DAY

WHEN WE "GET EMOTIONAL" WE OFTEN PUT OUR HANDS ON OUR HEARTS. SONGWRITERS WOULD LIKE US TO BELIEVE THAT THE HEART IS THE CENTER OF EMOTION. IN REALITY, EMOTIONS ARE CONTROLLED BY STRUCTURES IN THE HYPOTHALAMUS, IN THE BASAL FOREBRAIN AND IN THE BRAINSTEM.*

*SOURCE: WWW.PHARMJ.COM/INDEX.HTML

TODAY'S TOP 10
MAKE A LIST OF THE TOP TEN THINGS YOU GET EMOTIONAL ABOUT (ANY KIND OF EMOTION). JOURNAL ENTRY:
OKAY, I'M ON THE STARSHIP ENTERPRISE. I'M PROBABLY MORE LIKE (CHECK ONE) __CAPTAIN KIRK (MISTER EMOTIONAL) __MR. SPOCK (MISTER UNEMOTIONAL). IF JESUS WERE TO TRANSPORT ONTO THE BRIDGE HE WOULD TELL ME TO…

May God open your ears and your heart. May your understanding of his love come from your mind and your heart. May you listen with your entire self.

.10J

...hard to do, and not nearly as much fun as sharing them with others.

below the surface of the water...

urging your emotions is like holding beach balls down

Someone Just Like You

"God is so awesome!" Terry was in the middle of his testimony. "I just want to tell all of you that God is just so awesome! I've only been a Christian for about a year now, but I just can't believe how awesome God is! Every day I wake up and say, 'God, you are really awesome!' Hey, don't you all agree? I look around at the guys I used to run around with. I look at most of the kids on our campus, and I think to myself, God, you are really awesome! If all my friends could know how awesome God is, what a difference it would make. So I just want you to know how totally awesome God is!" ¶ When Terry sat down, Diane, the youth group skeptic, stood up. "Terry, I'm excited that you think God is great. But what exactly did you just say? I have no idea what you were talking about. You said God was awesome, but never once did you say why! You just kept repeating that God is awesome. To be honest, it sounded more like a cheer than a testimony. Forgive me, Terry; I don't mean to hurt your feelings or anything. You know I think you're a neat guy, but don't you think we have to have some reasons for our faith other than just repeating one word over and over again?" ¶ The youth group didn't know how to respond. Some were angry with Diane. Some had no idea what she was talking about. Some agreed with her, even though they didn't want to hurt Terry's feelings.

IN THE STORY

If you were in the group and the tension started to get a little thick, what would you say to Diane? To Terry?

ife Hint:

eleven.

Fear can suggest weakness or cowardice. Other times, though, being afraid is a good thing. There's a fine line between fear that comes from weakness and fear that respects strength. It's okay, for example, to be afraid of tornadoes, or hurricanes, or earthquakes, or even a furious squall. ¶ When his fearful disciples came to him in the middle of the storm, Jesus asked them to think about why they were afraid. As the disciples demonstrated, the best thing to do with a healthy fear is take it to the Lord. You can bet that whatever causes you to be afraid doesn't cause Jesus to be afraid…and that ought to make you afraid. ¶ Think about it. Being afraid is good when it activates all your senses, causes you to be cautious, gets your adrenaline pumping, and prepares you to respond to danger. ¶ Being afraid is also good when it causes you to recognize how big, powerful, and awesome God is. When the disciples are afraid of God, it's because they respect him. The disciples were afraid of Jesus many times, and that's one of the traits that made them good disciples.

Mark 4:35-41
How Do You Say "Freakin' Awesome" in Aramaic?

That day when evening came, he said to his disciples, "Let us go over to the other side." Leaving the crowd behind, they took him along, just as he was, in the boat. There were also other boats with him.

A furious squall came up, and the waves broke over the boat, so that it was nearly swamped. Jesus was in the stern, sleeping on a cushion. The disciples woke him and said to him, "Teacher, don't you care if we drown?"

He got up, rebuked the wind and said to the waves, "Quiet! Be still!" Then the wind died down and it was completely calm. He said to his disciples, "Why are you so afraid? Do you still have no faith?"

They were terrified and asked each other, "Who is this? Even the wind and the waves obey him!"

FACT FOR THE DAY

STEPHEN KING SAID THE THINGS THAT SCARE US THE MOST ARE: FEAR FOR SOMEONE ELSE, FEAR OF OTHERS (PARANOIA), FEAR OF DEATH, FEAR OF INSECTS (ESPECIALLY SPIDERS, FLIES, AND BEETLES), FEAR OF CLOSED-IN PLACES, FEAR OF RATS, FEAR OF SNAKES, FEAR OF DEFORMITY, FEAR OF SQUISHY THINGS, AND OF COURSE, FEAR OF THE DARK.

TODAY'S TOP 10

MAKE A LIST OF THE TOP TEN THINGS YOU ARE IN "AWE" OF.

JOURNAL ENTRY:

THE LAST TIME I REALLY FELT LIKE I WAS DOING WHAT GOD WANTED ME TO DO I…

fear

Someone Just Like You

Life is hard in what's left of Cheryl's family. She's a city girl whose single mom has no time to take her camping or hiking in the mountains. In fact, her mom has no time for hardly anything except working. She seems to work all the time, and Cheryl has to work weekends and help out. It's not exactly a bad life, but it's hard—not much money. Not much free time, not many relationships, no vacations, and no time to herself. She hasn't seen her dad in five years; though, frankly, she has no desire to see him or communicate with him. Cheryl feels distant from most people. She doesn't really have time for romantic relationships either, but then most of the guys she knows are clueless about responsibility and commitment. ¶ The bright light in Cheryl's life is the church. Her mom makes sure they both have time for church and youth group, which she looks forward to every week. She's not just in it for the spiritual growth; for Cheryl, youth group is a wonderful distraction from her everyday routine. ¶ Last week was the most amazing experience she ever had. Somehow she and her mom had saved up enough money for Cheryl to go to the church summer retreat. She'd never been to camp before; heck, she'd never been to the mountains before for any reason. One night she snuck out of her cabin to sleep under the stars. She had never seen so many stars, never seen so much beauty. As Cheryl stared at the sky she felt a strange surge of emotion. Her eyes filled with tears as she realized for the first time just how huge the universe was, how magnificent God's creation was, and how small she was. She'd heard all this as a little kid in Sunday school, but somehow this bigness and her smallness—and God's love for her—seemed overwhelming. Cheryl began crying.

It was then she became afraid. *What's the matter with me, she thought. Am I losing it? God is much bigger than I ever imagined, and I am just a nobody, a nothing. Why should this God care about me? What if I mess up? What will happen to me if I really give my life to a God this big? Why do I feel so scared?* ¶ Cheryl fell asleep crying. Camp ended the next day, but Cheryl still hasn't recovered. She's afraid to talk to anyone about her experience. She's beginning to wonder if there is something wrong with her.

IN THE STORY

If Cheryl came to you and spilled out all of the things she was thinking and stressing over...

Friendliness is kind, trustworthy, and loyal. A disciple is more than a follower, more than a learner. A disciple is a friend, a confidant, someone who is trusted, a companion, and a person who comes alongside. Friends share their lives with each other, talk about everything, and reveal their deepest secrets. Friends know how to listen, and they know how to be with each other without saying a word. Friends do not just care for a common cause; they care for each other. ¶ Disciples follow Jesus' teachings; friends follow Jesus' heart. Disciples will die for the truth; friends will die for each other. Disciples spend a lot of time together, getting to know each other, and building their relationship—not just their beliefs. Disciples who are friends know the meaning of relationship and community. They understand that Christianity is not an isolated adventure; it involves making friends with the friends of Jesus.

John 15:11-17
Jesus explains being a true disciple.

"I have told you this so that my joy may be in you and that your joy may be complete. My command is this: Love each other as I have loved you. Greater love has no one than this, that he lay down his life for his friends. You are my friends if you do what I command. I no longer call you servants, because a servant does not know his master's business. Instead, I have called you friends, for everything that I learned from my Father I have made known to you. You did not choose me, but I chose you and appointed you to go and bear fruit—fruit that will last. Then the Father will give you whatever you ask in my name. This is my command: Love each other."

12.

TODAY'S TOP 10
MAKE A LIST OF THE TOP TEN FRIENDS OF YOURS...NOT IN ORDER. (LEAVE SPACE FOR JESUS, GOD, AND YOUR OWN NAME, IF YOU'D LIKE.)

JOURNAL ENTRY:
IT'S TIME FOR "COOKING WITH CHRIST." TODAY IN THE KITCHEN YOU AND JESUS ARE MAKING A DISH CALLED "FRIENDSHIP." THIS IS THE RECIPE...

FACT FOR THE DAY

THE WORDS TO THE HYMN "WHAT A FRIEND WE HAVE IN JESUS" WERE WRITTEN BY JOSEPH SCRIVEN IN 1855. HE WROTE THEM FOR HIS MOTHER WHO LIVED IN IRELAND. THE WORDS WERE LATER PAIRED WITH THE TUNE FROM A SONG CALLED "WHEN THIS BLOODY WAR IS OVER" IN 1868.

Life Hint: When everything in your life goes wrong, look beside you. The one who didn't leave is your friend.

May God grant you friendship beyond your imagination; may you show it to someone else; may you feel it in Jesus; and may you find it in yourself.

IN THE STORY
Imagine you bump into Greg at the grocery store.
What would you say?

Someone Just Like You

First Church's youth pastor was really cool. He was funny, good-looking, a great communicator, and a lover of Jesus. Everyone liked Greg and his wife, Lindy. Greg spent hours just hanging out with us kids. He was really fun to be around. He was always teasing and joking and generally being the center of attention, which no one minded because he knew how to show us a good time. And when it came to talking about Jesus, you could tell Greg really cared about us. He had such a passion for Jesus that you couldn't help but want the same thing. ¶ I don't know how many times Greg had the youth group in tears because of our lack of commitment. Secretly, I think all of us wanted to be just like Greg. He was so happy, so on fire, so cool. He used to tell us that he and his wife didn't need adult friends because the youth group kids were his friends.

¶ Then the news broke about his affair. At first none of us believed it. It was crazy. It had to be a bunch of lies. Greg disappeared for a couple weeks, but we were sure that he would come back and that the whole affair thing would be disproved. But Greg never came back. Slowly the ugly facts were made known. It turned out Greg not only was having an affair with one of the girls in our group, he had run off with her (though she was barely 18), leaving his wife devastated and alone.

¶ At first we were shocked, then we got angry. We would sit around for hours trying to figure out what went wrong. Sure, we don't know the whole story, but we knew one thing: Greg was real— a stranger to us, a loner. He had no friends, really. He said we were his friends, but he never talked to us about his life, and he never let us talk to him about ours. He preached to us, but he was far from a friend. We remembered that he said he didn't need adult friends. Now we know why. Friends know you, and if he'd had a friend, his affair would've been found out in the beginning. ¶ I'm sure there's much more to the story than this. Our youth group is in shambles. We've tried to be there for Lindy, but it's kind of awkward. We heard she's going to another church. None of us will ever be the same after this betrayal, but I'll tell you one thing: we sure have become good friends.

friendliness

generosity

Generous disciples are more than doers; they are givers. Yet disciples give more than words and knowledge to others; disciples give themselves to others. Disciples serve others by listening, supporting, encouraging, affirming, confronting, helping, loving, empathizing, and being there. Disciples are generous with their time and energy, imitating the One who knew how to serve. As servants, disciples learn how to be sensitive, to know when they're needed and when they're not. True servants can read people well. They can feel pain in others and know when to step in and help. True servanthood is very difficult, yet very important, because it's the one unmistakable way people recognize Jesus in us (Matthew 25:34-46).

2 Corinthians 9:6-11
The more you give the more you get.

Remember this: Whoever sows sparingly will also reap sparingly, and whoever sows generously will also reap generously. Each man should give what he has decided in his heart to give, not reluctantly or under compulsion, for God loves a cheerful giver. And God is able to make all grace abound to you, so that in all things at all times, having all that you need, you will abound in every good work. As it is written: "He has scattered abroad his gifts to the poor; his righteousness endures forever."

Now he who supplies seed to the sower and bread for food will also supply and increase your store of seed and will enlarge the harvest of your righteousness. You will be made rich in every way so that you can be generous on every occasion, and through us your generosity will result in thanksgiving to God.

FACT FOR THE DAY
IN 1999, BILL AND MELINDA GATES MADE THE LARGEST DONATION TO CHARITY IN HISTORY. THE COUPLE DONATED 3.4 BILLION DOLLARS TO WORLDWIDE HEALTH AND EDUCATION CHARITIES.

JOURNAL ENTRY:

WHAT WAS THE MOST UNSELFISH THING YOU'VE EVER DONE? WRITE ABOUT ONE THING YOU DID FOR SOMEONE ELSE WITH ABSOLUTELY NO THOUGHT FOR YOURSELF.

May God grant you the gift of being a servant. May you truly know that it is in giving that we receive.

TODAY'S TOP 10
MAKE A LIST OF THE TOP TEN THINGS YOU'VE GIVEN AWAY.

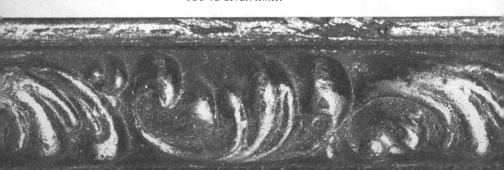

Every month Daryl's youth group went to Beverly Manor to put on a church service for the old people who lived there. Daryl didn't like to go, but he felt obligated. That's what Jesus would do, Daryl thought, even though Jesus didn't have old-folks homes in his day. Lucky him! ¶ Though Daryl had gone to five services at the Manor, he never really did anything. He just stood in the back of the room and held the hand of an old man. The man's name was Oliver, and he seldom spoke. He must've been in his eighties or nineties. Most of the time he slept through the church service. Daryl liked the old guy, though. He used to wake him up and talk to him, even though Oliver never seemed like he was listening. When Daryl would get ready to leave, though, Oliver seemed to know and would squeeze Daryl's hand. Daryl never told anyone about this, but each time he started to leave and felt Oliver squeeze his hand, he would lean down and whisper in his ear, "I'm sorry, Oliver, I have to go; but I love you and I'll be back next month. I promise." ¶ On his sixth visit to the Manor, Daryl was looking forward to seeing Oliver again. But Oliver wasn't around. As the service began, Daryl became concerned. He said to the head nurse, "I don't see Oliver here today. Is he okay?" ¶ The nurse asked Daryl to follow her to Room 13, where Oliver lay in bed, looking frail and near death. Oliver's eyes were closed and his breathing was irregular. Daryl walked over and grabbed Oliver's hand. He had never seen anyone dying before, and he had a difficult time holding back his tears. Daryl sat with Oliver for an hour. When Daryl started to leave, he knew he might not ever see Oliver again. Oliver squeezed his hand. Oliver knew, too. Daryl said what he always said: "I'm sorry, Oliver, I have to go, but I love you." ¶ When Daryl walked out of the room, a young woman was standing there waiting for him. "Hello," she said. "I'm Oliver's granddaughter. He's dying, you know."

¶ "Yes, I know," Daryl said. ¶ "I wanted to meet you," she said. "See, I came to see my grandfather when the doctors said he was dying. They said he couldn't talk, but he could always talk to me. Last week he sort of woke up and said to me, 'Please say goodbye to Jesus for me.' I told him that he was going to be with Jesus soon. He looked at me with the most alert eyes I've ever seen and said, 'I know, but he comes to see me every month, and he might not know I've gone.' I asked the nurse if she had any idea what he meant, and she told me that you came once a month and held his hand. I wanted to thank you for him…and for me—and, well, I imagine Jesus is very glad to have been mistaken for you." ¶ Oliver died in his sleep that evening.

IN THE STORY
Imagine you are Daryl. What would you say to
Oliver's granddaughter?

Life Hint:
Mother Teresa once said: We can do no great things, only small things with great love.

hatred.

Hatred can come in the form of criticism, ridicule, or sarcasm. It can take the shape of rejection, hostility, or avoidance. Those who hate you find ways to hurt you, ways to make you feel stupid, ways to make it look as though you're at fault. Hateful people know how to convince everyone around them that they are your friends while they slowly twist knives in your back. ¶ Hatred can take the form of "godly" behavior as well. People can hide behind their religion and use it as a weapon to demolish you and your reputation. Hatred is pure evil. It can destroy people very quickly. What is frightening about hatred is that those who hate feel no remorse. They feel good. They feel righteous and legitimate. They feel justified in their hatred. Good people are often most hurt because they're not prepared for how vicious and ugly hatred can be. Hatred can be triggered quickly when people feel threatened or in danger of losing power. Jesus made it very clear that people are capable of hating nice, godly disciples just as they were capable of hating the sinless, loving Son of God.

John 15:18-25

Next time you feel like someone hates you, check your hands. See nail scars? Then you got off easy.

VOTION.

Today's TOP 10
MAKE A LIST OF THE TOP TEN THINGS YOU'VE SEEN HATE DO.

JOURNAL ENTRY:

HAVE YOU EVER BEEN HATED? DESCRIBE HATE IN A PHYSICAL SENSE. WHAT DOES IT LOOK LIKE? SOUND LIKE? SMELL LIKE? FEEL LIKE? HAVE YOU EVER DONE THAT TO SOMEONE ELSE?

"If the world hates you, keep in mind that it hated me first. If you belonged to the world, it would love you as its own. As it is, you do not belong to the world, but I have chosen you out of the world. That is why the world hates you. Remember the words I spoke to you: 'No servant is greater than his master.' If they persecuted me, they will persecute you also. If they obeyed my teaching, they will obey yours also. They will treat you this way

"Get outta my face!!!" Jesse's dad was an alcoholic, and right now he was coming down from one of his binges. The binge would usually start with Jessie's father verbally abusing anyone in sight. Eventually, as he drank more, he would leave for three or four days (which was a relief for everyone). Then he would return home remorseful, guilt-ridden, crying, vowing never to drink again. It was unusual for Jesse's dad to use such language when he was coming off a binge. ¶ "Dad, no way am I leavin'!" Jesse said. "I am trying to tell you that Jesus is the only one who can help you. I know. I started drinking my junior year and realized it was a black hole. A friend of mine told me about Jesus, and I stopped. You can stop, too, and you need to stop before you lose all of us." ¶ "Look, Billy Graham," his dad replied. "I don't need you telling me what to do. I don't need some TEENAGER tellin' ME he knows more than I do about life. You seem to forget that my dad was a preacher! He loved Jesus, all right, but he also loved his bottle. The only difference between him and me is that he was able to hide it from all those 'good church people.' Jesus didn't help my dad, he ain't going to help me, and he ain't helping you. Just because you haven't had a drink for a few days don't mean nothing. And you know what else, son? Religion is a bunch of crap, and no son of mine is going to become some Bible-toting fanatic. You got it?" ¶ "Dad, I just want you to get some help," Jesse said. ¶ "No you don't," his dad corrected. "You just want me to get out of here so you can run things and make everyone in the family a Jesus freak. Let me make it as clear as I can for you, son. I hate God, and I hate religion. All it did for me was pay for my father's booze. You keep going down this Jesus trail and I'll tell you right now, boy, I'll end up hating you, too. If you cared about me, you wouldn't have anything to do with Jesus. Period."

IN THE STORY

Imagine you are Jesse's minister and he asked you to go visit his dad. What would your first words be?

DEVOTION

because of my name, for they do not know the One who sent me. If I had not come and spoken to them, they would not be guilty of sin. Now, however, they have no excuse for their sin. He who hates me hates my Father as well. If I had not done among them what no one else did, they would not be guilty of sin. But now they have seen these miracles, and yet they have hated both me and my Father. But this is to fulfill what is written in their Law: 'They hated me without reason.'"

May you never know the damage of hate; but if you do,
may God shield you from its jagged edge and heal the scars that it has caused you.

humanity

May the God who created you just the way you are, help you on your journey to be the you that you want to be.

Humanity is normal. When you decide to follow Christ, you may leave your past behind, but you bring with you your friends, your family, and your humanity—complete with idiosyncrasies and flaws. When you bring yourself to Jesus, that self is attached to a whole lot of stuff—your physical looks, for example, and your emotional makeup, and personality, and family, and financial situation. ¶ This stuff complicates your decision to follow Jesus. For example, say you have a quick temper. So when you decide to follow Jesus, the "you" that follows Jesus also has a quick temper (kind of like Peter). Or you may have an alcoholic parent. Now that you're a Christian, you still have an alcoholic parent—or an overprotective mother, or a ridiculously strict stepfather, or a redneck brother. ¶ If your family was in any way weird before you decided to follow Christ, it's still weird after Jesus comes into your life. James and John had an aggressive mother who wanted her boys to have the best, who felt she had to look out for her "little boys." James and John simply had to deal with this uncomfortable reality. Jesus had to deal with it, too.

Matthew 20:20-28
You think your mom embarrasses you?

Then the mother of Zebedee's sons came to Jesus with her sons and, kneeling down, asked a favor of him. "What is it you want?" he asked.

She said, "Grant that one of these two sons of mine may sit at your right and the other at your left in your kingdom."

"You don't know what you are asking," Jesus said to them.

"Can you drink the cup I am going to drink?"

"We can," they answered.

Jesus said to them, "You will indeed drink from my cup, but to sit at my right or left is not for me to grant. These places belong to those for whom they have been prepared by my Father."

When the ten heard about this, they were indignant with the two brothers. Jesus called them together and said, "You know that the rulers of the Gentiles lord it over them, and their high officials exercise authority over them. Not so with you. Instead, whoever wants to become great among you must be your servant, and whoever wants to be first must be your slave—just as the Son of Man did not come to be served, but to serve, and to give his life as a ransom for many."

TODAY'S TOP 10

MAKE A LIST OF THE TOP TEN BIGGEST
MISTAKES YOU'VE EVER MADE.

JOURNAL ENTRY:

NO ONE IS PERFECT. CHOOSE ONE THING
ABOUT YOU THAT IS NOT PERFECT, AND
WRITE DOWN ALL THE WONDERFUL THINGS
ABOUT IT THAT YOU CAN THINK OF.

Someone Just Li

Jon is one of those students who dreads school. Every day he's forced to attend a place where, in his experience, each class, each homework assignment, almost every interaction is negative. Jon has been tested, retested, and retested again. Experts examined him for dyslexia, then vision problems, then hearing problems. It turns out that Jon is just a slow learner...whatever that means. Of course, having someone tell you that you learn slowly doesn't help much. In fact, it makes things worse. Now everyone knows Jon is a slow learner. At school he's treated with pity and sympathy instead of like a normal person—which he is, other than the fact that it takes him longer to learn than others. ¶ One week

a friend invited Jon to church the next Sunday. He actually liked the kids in the youth group. They accepted him, and he wasn't put into situations where his "slow learner" stuff was obvious. Not long afterwards Jon decided to become a Christian. The youth pastor had been saying for months that Jesus would not only save Jon's soul, but would be the answer to his problems. Jon still remembers the night he said yes to Jesus. The next day he felt like he was walking on air. He breezed through school and began to believe that because of his new faith, his problems would disappear—especially his slow learning. For three months Jon grew in his faith like crazy. He went to weekly Bible studies, shared his faith with others, and even got along with his parents better. Jon just knew that with Jesus his schoolwork would turn around. ¶ About that time Jon received an urgent referral from his school. The counseling department recommended that Jon be held back a year and reassigned to a special learning class. ¶ Thanks a lot, Jesus, Jon thought bitterly. You really know how to solve my problems.

FACT FOR THE DAY

THE PHILOSOPHER LUCY VAN
PELT ONCE SAID, "HUMANITY
I LOVE. IT'S PEOPLE I CAN'T
STAND."

IN THE STORY

Knowing this history, what would you say to John on his first day of school the next year?

Hunger goes beyond desire. Hunger for truth is a longing, a yearning...just as powerful as being hungry for food. Those who sincerely want to know more, to grow more, are driven by their passion for truth. A disciple is much more than a student or apprentice. A disciple isn't satisfied with knowing more. A disciple wants to know it all, to experience it all.

HUNGER 16

Disciples' longing for truth makes them willing learners, eager followers, with an insatiable hunger for knowledge. That hunger is aggressive, pursuing, and relentless. Hungry disciples are energized by their appetite and eagerly enlist others to search for truth with them. When you lose your appetite for truth, when you stop being hungry for God, then you become comfortable and lazy. Hunger is a quality that is central to what a disciple is.

John 6:25-35

How badly would you want to see grass after living at the North Pole for a year?

When they found him on the other side of the lake, they asked him, "Rabbi, when did you get here?"

Jesus answered, "I tell you the truth, you are looking for me, not because you saw miraculous signs but because you ate the loaves and had your fill. Do not work for food that spoils, but for food that endures to eternal life, which the Son of Man will give you. On him God the Father has placed his seal of approval."

Then they asked him, "What must we do to do the works God requires?"

Jesus answered, "The work of God is this: to believe in the one he has sent."

So they asked him, "What miraculous sign then will you give that we may see it and believe you? What will you do? Our forefathers ate the manna in the desert; as it is written: 'He gave them bread from heaven to eat.'"

Jesus said to them, "I tell you the truth, it is not Moses who has given you the bread from heaven, but it is my Father who gives you the true bread from heaven. For the bread of God is he who comes down from heaven and gives life to the world."

"Sir," they said, "from now on give us this bread."

Then Jesus declared, "I am the bread of life. He who comes to me will never go hungry, and he who believes in me will never be thirsty."

TODAY'S TOP 10
MAKE A LIST OF THE TOP TEN THINGS YOU REALLY WANT OUT OF LIFE. (NOT THE SUNDAY SCHOOL ANSWER, BUT WHAT DO YOU REALLY WANT?)

FACT FOR THE DAY

KRISPY KREME DOUGHNUTS
WAS ESTABLISHED IN 1937 IN
WINSTON, N.C. THE DOUGH-
NUTS WERE SO POPULAR THAT
THEY CUT A HOLE IN THE WALL
OF THE FACTORY TO SELL THEM
BY THE DOZEN. TODAY, MANY
PEOPLE HAVE UNCONTROLLABLE
CRAVINGS EVERY TIME THEY SEE
THE NEON "HOT DOUGHNUTS
NOW" LIGHT IN THE SKY.

Trina is confused. She used to attend Bible study every week and youth group every Sunday night. She loved learning about God and was thinking seriously about attending a Bible college when she graduates next year. But during the summer she found a good job as a waitress at a trendy restaurant. Because Trina looked much older than her 18 years and the customers liked her, the owners of the restaurant liked her. The money she made was so good, in fact, that she convinced her dad to let her buy a car. When school began, though, Trina needed to work weekends to keep up with her car payments. The rest of the time she spent trying to maintain her 4.0 GPA. It wasn't easy. Something had to go. ¶ One night on her way to work, she realized church and youth group didn't sound all that good anymore. So she stopped going. It certainly promised to make Trina's schedule easier. Now, three months later, she figured that all that "get on fire for God" stuff had begun to turn her off, anyway. And she began to dread the Bible like she dreaded the dentist. ¶ What's crazy is that Trina was so into God just three months ago. She was reading her Bible, praying for her friends, and thinking about the Lord all the time. She didn't think her enthusiasm for God would ever change. But it had. ¶ *Oh well, Trina thought. As soon as my senior year is over, I'll get back into my faith. Right now I need to pay my bills and keep my grades up. That's the most important issue for me.*

IN THE STORY Write a note of encouragement that you could

slip into Trina's locker.

May God give you just enough to satisfy your hunger but not enough to satisfy your cravin
May you continue to seek and find and seek again.

JOURNAL ENTRY:

REACHING THE DESTINATION ISN'T USUALLY
AS REWARDING AS THE JOURNEY. SOME OF THE
"JOURNEYS" I'M STILL WORKING ON INCLUDE...

SEVEN

THE WORLD'S LARGEST WATER
RIDE IS IN SANTA CLAUS,
INDIANA. THE ZOOMBABWE IS
102 FEET HIGH AND 887 FEET
LONG. PLUS THE WHOLE RIDE IS
DONE IN A PITCH-BLACK TUNNEL.

> May God grant you courage to step out of the boat. May you use this time
> in your life to gather as much as you can and carry it with you always.

immaturity

Immaturity can mean foolish, naive, silly, and childish. When people want to criticize a young person, they often use a word like immature to communicate dissatisfaction with certain kinds of behavior. Immaturity usually means people are not behaving appropriately, not "acting their age," not acting grown up. Often you'll hear an adult yell in exasperation, "Grow up!" by which the adult usually means, "Quit acting like a kid!" ¶ But immaturity is not always bad. It suggests being young, enthusiastic, energetic, undeveloped, inexperienced, or uninformed. Sometimes our immaturity is what causes us to try new ways of living, new ways of thinking, and new ways of believing. Immaturity often drives us to try new things, to risk more, to live fearlessly, even dangerously. Immaturity produces adventures, accidents, wild surprises, and humiliating failure. ¶ All of Jesus' disciples were immature. You have to be immature before you can be mature. It was during their immature years that the disciples did the most, learned the most, and put their lives in the most danger.

Matthew 14:22-33

Immediately Jesus made the disciples get into the boat and go on ahead of him to the other side, while he dismissed the crowd. After he had dismissed them, he went up on a mountainside by himself to pray. When evening came, he was there alone, but the boat was already a considerable distance from land, buffeted by the waves because the wind was against it.

During the fourth watch of the night Jesus went out to them, walking on the lake. When the disciples saw him walking on the lake, they were terrified. "It's a ghost," they said, and cried out in fear.

But Jesus immediately said to them: "Take courage! It is I. Don't be afraid."

"Lord, if it's you," Peter replied, "tell me to come to you on the water."

"Come," he said.

Then Peter got down out of the boat, walked on the water and came toward Jesus. But when he saw the wind, he was afraid and, beginning to sink, cried out, "Lord, save me!"

Immediately Jesus reached out his hand and caught him. "You of little faith," he said, "why did you doubt?"

And when they climbed into the boat, the wind died down. Then those who were in the boat worshiped him, saying, "Truly you are the Son of God."

Jesus does not sit in the boat and say, "Go." He stands out on the water and says, "Come."

Someone Just Like You

Marlena was very frustrated. Here she was, 16 years old, standing in front of the leaders of her church, and she could tell they were angry with her. All she did was stand up in the annual meeting to ask why the church was moving out of the inner city to the suburbs. The meeting was being held to approve the new plan to buy a piece of property in a beautiful area just outside of town. Someone had donated a few million dollars for the church to move out of the crime-infested, rapidly deteriorating old part of town. ¶ Marlena's family lived just a few blocks from where the new church would be built, but she still couldn't understand the decision. "Listen to me, please, everyone. I know I'm young. I know what I give to the church is a drop in the bucket. I know I'm just a kid, but we can't do this. We can't abandon this part of the city. Think of what we could do with the millions of dollars we're talking about if we invested it in the people who live all around us!" ¶ The minister stood to his feet. "Thanks, Marlena, we really do appreciate your input, but when you get older you'll understand. Dr. Kerry Dawson is a long-time member of this church, and his very gracious offer of three million dollars was made on the condition that we move. It would be a sin to turn down that amount of money."

¶ "But, Pastor," Marlena said tearfully, "why don't we just ask him to give the money here instead?" ¶ The entire congregation laughed. The vote was nearly unanimous to take the money and move. Marlena cast the only "no" vote.

IN THE STORY   If you were a member of the church, what would you say to Marlena in the parking lot after the meeting?

TODAY'S **TOP 10**
MAKE A LIST OF THE TOP TEN PEOPLE
WHO "GET" THE WHOLE "BEING
A CHILD" THING...

JOURNAL ENTRY:

THERE WAS THIS ONE TIME WHEN I
REALLY FELT LIKE I WAS ACTING LIKE
(OR BEING TREATED LIKE) A GROWN-UP...

incapable?

Incapable means you're unable to do something you want to do. It means you're in over your head, trapped by your circumstances, bewildered, confused, or just plain lost. Sometimes people are incapable because they haven't been trained properly, they don't possess the necessary skills, or they don't have enough experience. ¶ In the story below the disciples had just come down from a mountain where they had an unbelievable experience. They'd seen Jesus become transparent right in front of them! Not only that, they'd seen Moses and Elijah appear right in front of their eyes! What an experience! They were on top of the world. Then they came down the mountain and couldn't heal a little boy. They were frustrated, of course, but Jesus pointed out that healing little boys takes a lot of faith and a lot of time. Not everyone can heal little boys. The power comes from God, but the faith usually comes from us. Our response is the key.

¶ Disciples can't do everything. Being a disciple doesn't guarantee success. Disciples have to learn and work and spend a lot of time alone with Jesus. Being incapable doesn't mean we can't be a disciple, it just means we have a lot to learn.

THE DEEPEST PLACE TO BE IN OVER YOUR HEAD IS IN THE PACIFIC OCEAN. ITS DEEPEST POINT IS 36,200 FEET DEEP.*

FACT FOR THE DAY

*SOURCE: WWW.ENCHANTED-LEARNING.COM

TODAY'S **TOP 10**
MAKE A LIST OF THE TOP TEN THINGS YOU CAN'T DO.

JOURNAL ENTRY:
WHEN WE FELL AS TODDLERS, OUR PARENTS DID NOT SAY, "STAND UP! DON'T FALL LIKE THAT ANYMORE! WHAT'S WRONG WITH YOU?" THERE ARE MANY THINGS I WANT TO BE GOOD AT SOME DAY, AND SO...

Matthew 17:14-20
Why can't we do better?

When they came to the crowd, a man approached Jesus and knelt before him. "Lord, have mercy on my son," he said. "He has seizures and is suffering greatly. He often falls into the fire or into the water. I brought him to your disciples, but they could not heal him."

"O unbelieving and perverse generation," Jesus replied, "how long shall I stay with you? How long shall I put up with you? Bring the boy here to me." Jesus rebuked the demon, and it came out of the boy, and he was healed from that moment.

Then the disciples came to Jesus in private and asked, "Why couldn't we drive it out?"

He replied, "Because you have so little faith. I tell you the truth, if you have faith as small as a mustard seed, you can say to this mountain, 'Move from here to there' and it will move. Nothing will be impossible for you."

During the last two years, Sue had watched her friend Darci become very active in a local church, attend Bible studies every week, and really try to live her faith. Sue, on the other hand, wasn't a Christian and didn't think the "Jesus thing" was for her. Because of things that had happened in her life, she just didn't feel like God would accept her.

Someone Just Like You

¶ Darci was especially happy today. She had just returned from a church retreat and was going on and on about her relationship with God. Darci looked Sue straight in the eye, and said, "Sue, we've been friends now for two years. You've seen what Jesus has done in my life. Why don't you see what Jesus can do in yours?" ¶ Sue could feel the knot in her stomach. "Because, Darci, I…I…don't think God would have me."

¶ "What?" Darci started. "Why would you say that, Sue? Why…" ¶ Sue interrupted. "Because my dad has sexually abused me since I was 13, and I can't stop him! What is wrong with me, Darci? I'm a very messed-up person, and no one knows. I just can't tell anyone—my mother, the police, nobody! If this all came out, it would wreck my family. What can I do, Darci?" ¶ Darci was stunned. The words just caught in her throat. She didn't know what to say or do. ¶ "Come on, Darci," Sue continued, "tell me what to do. Where is your God, anyway? Why is this happening to me? Come on, help me!" ¶ Darci couldn't move. Never in a million years did she expect this from her friend. She was overwhelmed, confused, scared, hurting for her friend, but the words just wouldn't come. ¶ "Oh, thanks a lot, Darci," Sue said. "Thanks a lot. Yeah, God is great for people who have great lives like you. But he can't help people like me." ¶ Darci finally spoke. "No, Sue, that's not true. It's just that…" ¶ "Yeah, never mind, Darci," Sue said. "I could see it in your eyes. You don't know what to do with someone as messed up as me." Sue stormed off before Darci could say anything more. ¶ Darci burst into tears, confused, frustrated, and feeling like a failure. *Some Christian I am, she thought. Gosh, abused by her dad. I can't believe it. I know her parents—or at least I thought I did. I don't know what to say to Sue. I thought God would be here for me when something like this happened. So where are you, God?*

IN THE STORY What would you say to encourage Darci to try again?

May the God of patience be with you, watch over you, and pick you up when you fall, and may God be a light when you wander from the path.

Life Hint:
We don't have to know everything about God in order to love God.

independent means different, distinctive, unique, and self-confident. It does not require solitude, though. An independent disciple is still part of a community, but it means you don't need to rely on others to decide what God wants you to do. It means others who vehemently disagree with you don't intimidate you. Independent disciples are not shaken by disagreements or differing opinions.

¶ Independent people recognize that many times in life we have to go a different way than others. Different doesn't mean right, it just means different. Often two people can go separate ways and both be "right." Independence is not about being right; it's about going where God wants you to go. Barnabas and Paul strongly disagreed, but they both followed God, so they just went different directions. Independence is the active part of our uniqueness. Someone said it this way: "A disciple is independently dependent on God."

Acts 15:36-40
Different does not necessarily mean wrong:

Some time later Paul said to Barnabas, "Let us go back and visit the brothers in all the towns where we preached the word of the Lord and see how they are doing." Barnabas wanted to take John, also called Mark, with them, but Paul did not think it wise to take him, because he had deserted them in Pamphylia and had not continued with them in the work. They had such a sharp disagreement that they parted company. Barnabas took Mark and sailed for Cyprus, but Paul chose Silas and left, commended by the brothers to the grace of the Lord.

TODAY'S **TOP 10**

MAKE A LIST OF THE TOP TEN THINGS THAT SEPARATE YOU FROM THE CROWD (THESE CAN BE GOOD OR BAD).

JOURNAL ENTRY:

BEING A CHRISTIAN DOESN'T MAKE LIFE EASIER. IT MAKES IT HARDER. GOD HAS POINTED ME IN SOME BIZARRE DIRECTIONS. ONE TIME I...

FACT FOR THE DAY

DONALD SCHEER OF ATLANTA BOUGHT A PAINTING AT A FLEA MARKET FOR FOUR DOLLARS BECAUSE HE LIKED THE FRAME. LATER HE DISCOVERED AN ORIGINAL COPY OF THE DECLARATION OF INDEPENDENCE HIDDEN BEHIND THE CANVAS. HE SOLD THE COPY AT AN AUCTION FOR MORE THAN 2 MILLION DOLLARS.* WWW.SNOPES.COM

independence

The atmosphere was tense as Brad sat in front of his youth director's cluttered desk. "Brad, you are wasting the gifts you have. You are a great communicator; you work great with people; and I don't think God would give you those gifts and not want you to use them." ¶ "I know, Mike," Brad replied, "but I can write poetry, too, and that's what I really want to do. I'm good at it, and I feel so alive when I'm writing it." ¶ "Brad, feeling good is fine," Mike said, "but you have to make a living, you know. How many poets do you know who are making a living?" ¶ "You're kidding, right?" Brad asked. "Mike, you're the one who gets up in front of youth group each week and tells us making money sucks. Now you're all worried about money."

¶ "Brad," Mike responded. "I never said, 'Making money sucks.' I don't talk like that, for one thing. What I said was making a lot of money doesn't satisfy. But you have to eat, and you have to pay for an apartment. Besides, money has nothing to do with it. You have the gift of speaking. You should go into youth ministry. You should be helping in a youth group while you're going to school. While you're doing ministry you can write poetry in your spare time." ¶ "Oh, sure, in my spare time," Brad said. "Look, Mike, you're a great guy. You've really helped me through high school, and I respect you. But when it comes to my future, you're just plain wrong. I'm not going to do youth ministry. I'm not going to college this year. I'm going to travel to Europe. I'm going to write, and I'm going to read great poets. I think that's what God wants me to do." ¶ Mike looked at Brad for a long time. He responded quietly, "But, Brad, I've talked to your parents. In fact, they are the ones who asked me to talk to you. They think you're making a mistake, and, frankly, I agree with them. To be honest, Brad, you're not honoring your father and mother when you refuse to listen to them." ¶ Brad exploded inside. The whole deal was a setup. Mike had joined forces with Brad's mom and dad. Brad didn't say a word. He just stood up and left, knowing that if he opened his mouth he would say something very ugly. He was 18, old enough to make his own decisions, and that was what he was going to do. He wasn't disobeying his parents; he was obeying God!

Life Hint: Independence without dependence is like cooking a giant Thanksgiving dinner with all the trimmings and then eating it alone.

IN THE STORY

What's the difference between a dream and a pipe dream?

May you see the same God that is in you, in the one you most disagree with.

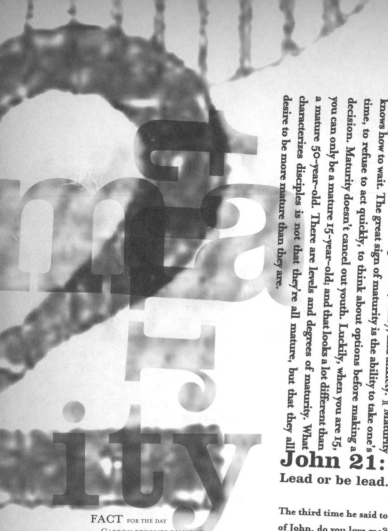

Maturity is what you get when you live for a while, have a lot of experiences (good and bad), and learn from those experiences. Maturity is not always measured by age. Young people can be mature; old people can be immature. Maturity is what causes disciples to make decisions based on deeper realities than feelings. Maturity is the opposite of impatience, worry, and anxiety. ¶ Maturity knows how to wait. The great sign of maturity is the ability to take one's time, to refuse to act quickly, to think about options before making a decision. Maturity doesn't cancel out youth. Luckily, when you are 15, you can only be a mature 15-year-old; and that looks a lot different than a mature 50-year-old. There are levels and degrees of maturity. What characterizes disciples is not that they're all mature, but that they all desire to be more mature than they are.

John 21:17-18
Lead or be lead.

The third time he said to him, "Simon son of John, do you love me?"

Peter was hurt because Jesus asked him the third time, "Do you love me?" He said, "Lord, you know all things; you know that I love you."

Jesus said, "Feed my sheep. I tell you the truth, when you were younger you dressed yourself and went where you wanted; but when you are old you will stretch out your hands, and someone else will dress you and lead you where you do not want to go."

FACT FOR THE DAY
CARBON BECOMES DIAMOND WHEN IT IS BENEATH 75 FEET OF ROCK AND HEATED TO TEMPERATURES OF MORE THAN 2000 DEGREES. HEAT AND PRESSURE WILL DO AMAZING THINGS.

TODAY'S **TOP 10**
MAKE A LIST OF THE TOP TEN THINGS WORTH WAITING FOR. (YES, YOU CAN WRITE DOWN *SEX* IF YOU WANT.)

JOURNAL ENTRY:

AS I LOOK BACK ON THE PERSON I WAS DURING THE HARDEST TIMES IN MY LIFE AND COMPARE THEM TO THE PERSON I AM NOW, I SEE THAT...

May God not solve your problems for you, but may God stand beside you as you go through them.

Someone Just Like You

Lincoln had a lot on his mind. With one month of school to go, his grades needed a boost. His dad had disappeared again and hadn't been seen for three weeks. His mom was exhausted from working two jobs. His older brother had been arrested for drug possession and was now out on bail. Life around the house was tense. To top it all off, he was getting squeezed from his church. Lincoln had developed some friendships with guys on the football team who went to the church where "everyone" went. Lincoln was one of the few black kids who came, and as a result he got a lot of attention.

¶ For the past six months, Lincoln had been attending a small-group Bible study, and it was good. He was learning a lot about Jesus. But now Lincoln's family needed him. Even though he was the younger brother, he was going to have to take responsibility. His small-group guys were praying for him and encouraging him to stay in the Bible study no matter what, but Lincoln knew better. He needed to work on his grades, and he needed to get a job to help his mom. No one at church agreed with his decision.

¶ "Look, Lincoln," they said, "Our church has big bucks. We'll get some money to help your family out. You need to keep close to Jesus and keep coming to youth group." It was weird, but Lincoln knew better. Deep inside he knew he needed to help his family himself and stay close to them. He loved Jesus; that wasn't going to change. But his family needed him, and he needed his family; so he made the decision to leave the small group. ¶ Next thing you know, everyone at Lincoln's church is ragging on him, harassing him, and telling him he's in danger of falling away from his faith. Instead of supporting him, people were dragging him down. Funny thing is, Lincoln feels really good about his decision. God seems even closer to Lincoln now than he did just a few weeks ago when life was much easier. Last night Lincoln fell asleep silently whispering, "Thank you, Jesus, for being here for me. You and me, God...we can do this!"

Life Hint:
Make up your own mind...there are a lot of people out there who are willing to make it up for you.

IN THE STORY Imagine you are Lincoln's youth minister and he has come to you with his feelings. What would you say?

ORDINARY. DAY 21.

Life Hint:
Whether you think you can or you can't...you're right.

FACT FOR THE DAY

THE OXFORD ENGLISH DICTIONARY, UNDER "ORDINARY," FIRST LISTS THE MEANINGS OF THE NOUN—SOMEONE WHO IS A JUDGE, A BOSS, IN AUTHORITY. THE SECOND MEANINGS (ADJECTIVE OR ADVERB) REFER TO NORMAL, EVERYDAY, COMMON TRAITS.

Ordinary means average, usual, plain, common, and typical. In other words, nothing special, nothing dazzling, and nothing spectacular. Just ordinary. ¶ Disciples are not known for their impressive credentials, their superior intellect, or their amazing giftedness. Disciples are just ordinary people who follow an extraordinary Lord. Disciples' power comes not from their charismatic personalities or their intellectual achievement; it comes from their powerlessness. ¶ What blows people away is how ordinary the followers of Jesus are and how much they can accomplish in their ordinariness. What also blows people away is how God chooses the ordinary. What distinguished the biblical disciples of Jesus more than anything else—and what astonished the crowds—was how plain they were. When it comes to following Jesus, being ordinary is one of the main qualifications.

1 Corinthians 1:26-31
There are no superheroes in the Scriptures.

Brothers, think of what you were when you were called. Not many of you were wise by human standards; not many were influential; not many were of noble birth. But God chose the foolish things of the world to shame the wise; God chose the weak things of the world to shame the strong. He chose the lowly things of this world and the despised things—and the things that are not—to nullify the things that are, so that no one may boast before him. It is because of him that you are in Christ Jesus, who has become for us wisdom from God—that is, our righteousness, holiness and redemption. Therefore, as it is written: "Let him who boasts boast in the Lord."

Today's TOP 10

MAKE A LIST OF THE TOP TEN THINGS THAT ARE FLAVORED WITH VANILLA.

JOURNAL ENTRY:

I CAN DO SO MANY THINGS THAT DON'T SEEM TO COUNT FOR MUCH. THE BIBLE SAYS GOD CAN TAKE THE ORDINARY AND MAKE IT EXTRAORDINARY. I BET GOD COULD TAKE MY...

Kirsten was your basic, ordinary girl. Even though she was a junior, she'd never had a date. Though many girls in her church would have been devastated to go through high school without a date, Kirsten didn't mind. She wasn't ready for all the entanglements of dating. She liked studying and reading. She liked having time to herself. ¶ Why Kirsten decided to go with the church youth group on a summer work trip is a mystery. She'd never even used a hammer before. Maybe it just sounded kind of fun to do something different. The trip to the worksite was a 10-hour drive from hell. The bus' air conditioning went out one hour into the trip. The bus itself broke down in the middle of the desert. Standing in 110-degree heat for three hours while a new bus came was not fun, but for some reason Kirsten didn't mind. She found herself energized by adversity. Most of the kids were complaining, wanting to go home, griping to the adult leaders, and generally pouting.

Someone Just Like You

¶ When the group arrived at the site five hours late, it took another three hours to set up camp in the dark. The next morning everyone was in a bad mood except Kirsten. Nobody noticed, though, because nobody ever noticed Kirsten. When they finally arrived at the building site, Kirsten found herself full of energy. She seemed to know what to do. While everyone was complaining about the heat and moping around, Kirsten was carrying wood, measuring, stacking tools, and getting ready for the real work of the day. ¶ Suddenly something inside Kirsten changed and she heard herself giving instructions to people. Not only was she telling kids what to do, she found herself encouraging others, bringing water to thirsty workers just when they needed it, and showing up just when someone needed help. She was amazing, and everyone began to notice. Kirsten was as surprised as anyone else. Quiet, shy Kirsten was supervising all the popular, sharp kids. It was just so out of character. Normally Kirsten never said a word. She just watched everyone else in the youth group. *Hmm,* Kirsten thought as she fell into her sleeping bag late that night, *not a bad day for a shy nerd.*

IN THE STORY

May God take your completely ordinary, everyday, walking-around existence and use it in ways you can't even imagine.

What would you say to Kirsten when you woke up the next day?

Overconfidence—we all experience this from time to time. When life is sweet, school is great, a new girlfriend or boyfriend has just come into the picture, and everything seems under control, it's difficult not to be overconfident. Overconfidence is the feeling that nothing can go wrong, that we are invincible, strong, and able to meet any challenge. ¶ The writer C S Lewis said that when everything is going great we can see God everywhere. He also said that when life is not great we can't find God anywhere. Often, though, when life is good we begin to take our eyes off God and start relying or depending on our own circumstances. Usually we're not aware of this shift in focus. The longer that life is good the easier it is to forget about God and rely on ourselves. Before we know it our thinking shifts from "God is so good" to "I am so cool," and then we're in trouble. ¶ Overconfidence tricks us into believing that nothing can derail us, defeat us, or corrupt us. But when that happens we're already corrupt. Here's the ugly truth: the only solution for overconfidence is humiliation. In other words, when you climb up a tower, the only way down is to fall. Falling off the tower of overconfidence is not fun, but more often than not it's a very effective way to get our focus back on Jesus.

Peter was happy to be the right-hand man until it got dangerous.

While Peter was below in the courtyard, one of the servant girls of the high priest came by. When she saw Peter warming himself, she looked closely at him. "You also were with that Nazarene, Jesus," she said. But he denied it. "I don't know or understand what you're talking about," he said, and went out into the entryway.

When the servant girl saw him there, she said again to those standing around, "This fellow is one of them." Again he denied it. After a little while, those standing near said to Peter, "Surely you are one of them, for you are a Galilean."

He began to call down curses on himself, and he swore to them, "I don't know this man you're talking about."

Immediately the rooster crowed the second time. Then Peter remembered the word Jesus had spoken to him: "Before the rooster crows twice you will disown me three times." And he broke down and wept.

Mark 14:66-72

Life Hint: Those who stand in the hurricane and bare the wind to blow them away are usually the ones who get hit with a flying tree.

SURVIVORS OF THE TITANIC WROTE IN THEIR DIARIES THAT THE CREWMEMBERS COULD BE HEARD REPEATING THE PHRASE "EVEN GOD COULDN'T SINK THIS SHIP." ON APRIL 15, 1912, IT SANK. SURVIVOR MARON SINNOTT WAS QUOTED AS SAYING, "IT'S NO MYSTERY. IT WAS ARROGANCE."

FACT FOR THE DAY

Tito sat in front of the stadium with the other graduates and smiled. Life was good. The last few years had been especially tough in the barrio. His brother was in jail for gang activity…his sister had been in and out of drugs and was finally doing better, though as a high school freshman she had a long way to go. The rock of the family was Tito, the one Mom and Dad were very proud of. He was the first to graduate from high school, and he would be the first child to attend college. The scholarship had come in, and his job was looking good for the summer. ¶ Tito knew where his strength had come from—God. Since he'd become a Christian, his life really had turned around. His youth director had rescued Tito from disaster often during his high school years, but this year God had stepped in big-time. Tito had kept his grades up and stayed out of trouble, and now he was reaping the rewards. Life was good. ¶ The only problem that lingered was his temper. It had been a year now since he'd been in a fight, but with God in his life he knew his fighting days were over. His temper had been calmed. After graduation Tito drove to meet his friends at the local McDonalds for lunch and a final celebration of a great year. On the way to McDonalds, rap music maxed out on his low-rider stereo, he was pulled over by a very arrogant police officer. ¶ "Out of the car and hands on the roof! Now!" ¶ Tito was taken by surprise. He could feel the anger building inside of him. *Come on*, he thought, *Stay calm. Jesus, I need your help.* ¶ He spoke to the cop as evenly as he could. "Hey, what's the problem, man? What'd I do?" ¶ "I don't need to tell you anything, Chico, except there's been a robbery and you look like the person who did it. Now out of the car." ¶ Tito's anger was building. "Excuse me, sir, but I don't like being called 'Chico,' and I was just at my graduation. I have lots of witnesses." ¶ "Listen, Chico, I don't have time to mess with you. Get out of the car and do as I said!" ¶ Tito lost it. "You can take your **** badge and shove it, pig!" ¶ Thirty minutes later, Tito, still furious, sat waiting for his parents at juvenile hall. The P.D. had apologized for the mistake, and he was going to be released to his parents. ¶ But Tito was mad at God for letting this happen—and mad at himself for losing his temper. Apparently his faith wasn't as life changing as he'd thought it was.

IN THE STORY   Write a note to Tito from his mother or father. What will you say?

Today's TOP 10

MAKE A LIST OF THE TOP TEN PEOPLE YOU KNOW WHO COULD STAND TO BE TAKEN DOWN A PEG OR TWO. (YES, YOU CAN USE CELEBRITIES OR POLITICIANS, BUT LEAVE THE NUMBER ONE SPACE BLANK.)

JOURNAL ENTRY:

THERE WAS THIS ONE TIME WHEN I WAS REALLY GETTING A LITTLE TOO COCKY, AND I WOUND UP…

May God keep you humble. May you remember that being a servant does make you better because your boss created the universe. May you find the truth in serving instead of being served.

JOURNAL ENTRY:

SOME OF THE HARDEST LESSONS I'VE
LEARNED CAME AS A RESULT OF SOME
AMAZING EXPERIENCES. THERE WAS THIS
ONE TIME...

TODAY'S TOP 10

MAKE A LIST OF THE TOP TEN LESSONS
YOU'VE LEARNED FROM EXPERIENCE,
NOT FROM A BOOK.

practical

Practical means down-to-earth, sensible, and realistic. People who are practical are simple, focused, and able to see what lies before them. A practical person says, "I could get my term paper done the night before it's due, but if anything goes wrong, I'm dead. If my computer crashes, if the power goes out, if I run out of paper at three in the morning, my assignment is doomed. So I'll start working on it a month in advance." ¶ A practical person says, "I might have enough will power to say no to sex if I watch videos at my girlfriend's house with her parents gone for the weekend, but I probably won't, so we'd better go someplace else." Practical people give God what they have instead of complaining about what they don't have. Practical people believe "something is better than nothing."

¶ Practical people don't sit back and ask God to do everything while they do nothing. Instead they do something and then ask God to bless that something. Practical disciples give God what they can and assume God will bless their gift.

John 6:5-13
The disciples get a lesson in project management

When Jesus looked up and saw a great crowd coming toward him, he said to Philip, "Where shall we buy bread for these people to eat?" He asked this only to test him, for he already had in mind what he was going to do.

Philip answered him, "Eight months' wages would not buy enough bread for each one to have a bite!" Another of his disciples, Andrew, Simon Peter's brother, spoke up, "Here is a boy with five small barley loaves and two small fish, but how far will they go among so many?"

Jesus said, "Have the people sit down." There was plenty of grass in that place, and the men sat down, about five thousand of them. Jesus then took the loaves, gave thanks, and distributed to those who were seated as much as they wanted. He did the same with the fish.

When they had all had enough to eat, he said to his disciples, "Gather the pieces that are left over. Let nothing be wasted." So they gathered them and filled twelve baskets with the pieces of the five barley loaves left over by those who had eaten.

"If God wants us to go to Brazil then we'll raise the $18,000—$6,000 each for three months of discipleship training in Ecuador," Brad said confidently. He and his two best friends in the youth group were looking forward to their mission experience during their last summer together before heading off to college. Brad, Dan, and Reggie were inseparable. They'd been close buddies since first grade. They decided to graduate early, take three months to raise their support, and head to Ecuador the first day of summer. All they needed to do, they decided, was make a presentation at church, send support letters to their family and friends, and see what would happen. They were confident God would provide. The church had already committed $6,000 ($2,000 each) and they knew the other $12,000 would come in.

¶ Since they were so sure God wanted them to go to Ecuador, all three decided there was no need for them to work. Instead they spent three months doing guy things—movies, camping, hiking, boating, and hanging out at the beach. With one month to go, the boys came together to count up the pledges of support. When they were finished counting, the boys couldn't believe the numbers. Including the church pledge, they had raised less than $12,000. They were $6,000 short of the amount they needed. They checked their list of those who hadn't responded yet and found only two names. They weren't going to have enough money. The boys were crushed. What had gone wrong? How could they have been so sure of God's leading and not have gotten the support they needed? Disappointed and angry with God, they called their youth director to ask him for advice on what to do next. ¶ "I think God does want you guys to go to Ecuador," Trina, their youth leader, said, "but you've blown it big time." ¶ "What are you talking about?" they asked. "We've contacted everyone we could think of." ¶ "I know. But if each of you had gotten a full-time job for the three months you've been out of school, you would have ended up with just enough. Instead you decided to play around these last few weeks, and now it's too late."

¶ The guys hung up the phone angry. "This is totally stupid," they agreed. "If God wanted us to go to Ecuador, he would've come through. He understands how important our friendship is." The guys talked long into the night and decided that God didn't want them to go on a mission project this summer. They sent all the money and pledges back, got part-time jobs at three fast food places at the beach, and spent the rest of the summer working on their tans and their friendship.

FACT FOR THE DAY
JIMMY BUFFET RELEASED HIS
DEBUT ALBUM IN 1970 ENTITLED
DOWN TO EARTH.

IN THE STORY Write a postcard from Trina to the boys back home.

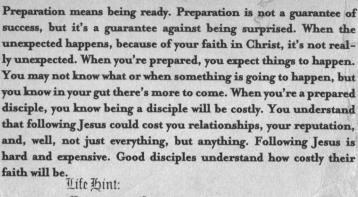

Preparation means being ready. Preparation is not a guarantee of success, but it's a guarantee against being surprised. When the unexpected happens, because of your faith in Christ, it's not really unexpected. When you're prepared, you expect things to happen. You may not know what or when something is going to happen, but you know in your gut there's more to come. When you're a prepared disciple, you know being a disciple will be costly. You understand that following Jesus could cost you relationships, your reputation, and, well, not just everything, but anything. Following Jesus is hard and expensive. Good disciples understand how costly their faith will be.

Life Hint:
Measure twice. Cut once.

FACT FOR THE DAY
THE BOY SCOUTS OF AMERICA
HAVE BEEN USING THE MOTTO
"BE PREPARED" SINCE 1910.

PREPA

TODAY'S **TOP 10**
MAKE A LIST OF THE TOP TEN
WORST BREAK-UP LINES.

Luke 14:28-35

Are you ready to follow Jesus? I mean really ready?

"Suppose one of you wants to build a tower. Will he not first sit down and estimate the cost to see if he has enough money to complete it? For if he lays the foundation and is not able to finish it, everyone who sees it will ridicule him, saying, 'This fellow began to build and was not able to finish.'

"Or suppose a king is about to go to war against another king. Will he not first sit down and consider whether he is able with ten thousand men to oppose the one coming against him with twenty thousand? If he is not able, he will send a delegation while the other is still a long way off and will ask for terms of peace. In the same way, any of you who does not give up everything he has cannot be my disciple.

"Salt is good, but if it loses its saltiness, how can it be made salty again? It is fit neither for the soil nor for the manure pile; it is thrown out.

"He who has ears to hear, let him hear."

JOURNAL ENTRY:

I THOUGHT, AS A CHRISTIAN,
I WOULD BE FULLY PREPARED
WHEN I.....

Don knew all about sex and its consequences. Before he became a Christian he'd been sexually involved with all of his girlfriends. His new girlfriend, Leslie, went to his church; and, although it had been difficult, Don had held the line on sexual activity. His youth director had warned him that being a Christian wasn't easy and that often we have difficulty at our weakest link. In the case of Don, the weakest link was sex. Sexual temptation for Don was extremely strong and alluring. Don could remember most of his sexual experiences. He wasn't proud of them; they haunted him, and they made it very hard for him not to get sexually involved with Leslie. The couple had been dating for a year now, and there had been no slip-ups. Don was starting to believe his commitment to Christ was taking hold. ¶ That's why Don was blindsided by Leslie's note. He was sitting in his bedroom, as he had been for the past hour, just staring at the note. He couldn't believe what he was reading. Leslie had slipped the note in his backpack. When he dropped her off at work, she said, "Oh, Don, I left you a note in your backpack. Don't read it until you get home." Because their one-year anniversary was coming up, he was getting excited about what she had to say.

¶ He rushed home, and ripped open the note:

¶ From the very beginning of our relationship I knew you were special. I loved you from the first time we started talking in English. I'd seen you at church a lot, but never really talked to you. When we finally connected I thought this would be forever. ¶ I know you love me, Don, and I love you, too. But I guess I've come to the conclusion I'm not the girl for you. I mean, I don't think I'm good enough for you. See, Don, I've always had a sexual relationship with the guys I've gone steady with, and from the beginning you made it clear you didn't want that with us. ¶ At first, I thought that was the coolest thing. I'd never dated a guy who didn't want to have sex. I guess secretly I believed we wouldn't have sex for a while, but once we knew we loved each other we would weaken and give in. But you haven't given in, and I can't believe I'm saying this, but it bothers me. ¶ I want more from a guy than just going places and talking. I want to feel like he wants me, all of me. I want to do more than feel close; I want to be close. I want what sex gives, I guess—more than I thought. ¶ So, Don, I really respect you and think you are cool, but I just don't think I'm good for you; so I want to break it off. I know this is news to you, but I've been thinking about it for a long time and I actually have another guy I've been seeing for awhile. I know you are probably hurt; but, Don, I'm sure God will help you find the right girl. I'm just not her.

May got grant you the patience it takes to make yourself ready to be a follower of Jesus. God knows it isn't easy and he's willing to wait.

DAY TWENTY-FOUR

speaking a LAND

Seeking is searching, probing, and stalking. Seekers aren't satisfied with secondhand experience. They want to see, to touch, to taste, and to know with all their senses what they are looking for. Seekers don't give up easily. They are persistent, unrelenting, fearless, and focused. I John's disciples were seeking the Messiah. John had talked about him and had identified Jesus as him. Suddenly the men who were disciples of John became disciples of Jesus. Their seeking caused them to follow Jesus, hang out with him, talk with him, and get to know him. It's interesting that the John who recorded the Bible passage below about the disciples' beginning with Jesus, wrote toward the end of his life, "That which was from the beginning, which we have heard, which we have seen with our eyes, which we have looked at and our hands have touched—this we proclaim" (1 John 1:1). Seekers settle for nothing less than the real thing. Seekers seek with their whole selves. And one other thing: true seekers find.

Life Hint:
Look. (Do that physically, emotionally, mentally, and spiritually).

The next day John was there again with two of his disciples. When he saw Jesus passing by, he said, "Look, the Lamb of God!"

When the two disciples heard him say this, they followed Jesus. Turning around, Jesus saw them following and asked, "What do you want?"

They said, "Rabbi" (which means Teacher), "where are you staying?"

"Come," he replied, "and you will see." So they went and saw where he was staying, and spent that day with him. It was about the tenth hour. Andrew, Simon Peter's brother, was one of the two who heard what John had said and who had followed Jesus. The first thing Andrew did was to find his brother Simon and tell him, "We have found the Messiah" (that is, the Christ). And he brought him to Jesus.

Jesus looked at him and said, "You are Simon son of John. You will be called Cephas" (which, when translated, is Peter).

John 1:35-42

FACT FOR THE DAY

ACCORDING TO AN EPISODE OF MONTY PYTHON'S FLYING CIRCUS THE LONGEST GAME OF HIDE AND SEEK LASTED 11 YEARS, 2 MONTHS, 9 HOURS, 3 MIN, AND 27.4 SECONDS.

You might just find what you are looking for.

STARE OUT YOUR WINDOW AND TRY TO
DESCRIBE WHAT YOU SEE AS IF YOU'VE
NEVER SEEN IT BEFORE. WHEN YOU'RE
DONE, DO THAT WITH YOUR LIFE.

TODAY'S **TOP 10**

MAKE A LIST OF THE TOP TEN THINGS
YOU'D ASK GOD IF YOU COULD MEET
HIM FACE TO FACE TODAY.

Someone Just Like You

Ever since I became a Christian, my life has been miserable. Here's the deal: a friend of mine brought me to a concert at his church. My folks were divorced when I was 13; and to be honest, I've never quite recovered. I live with my mom, and I love her a lot; but I do miss my dad, even though he ran off and married his secretary...but that's another story. ¶ So I went to this concert, which was really cool, and the lead singer talked about how he used to be on drugs and stuff, how his parents were all screwed up, and how he met Jesus and had his life turned around, and I said, "Yes!" he asked if anyone wanted to know Jesus like he did, and I said, "Yes!" ¶ I had no idea what trouble my faith was going to cause! I had a million questions. On the way home from the concert I was going crazy with questions. All my friends were excited that I had become a Christian, but they were totally clueless about my questions. They told me to talk to the youth director. The next day I did, and I still am. But I can tell he doesn't want to talk to me anymore. And I can tell that all the kids in the youth group are sick of my questions. I raise my hand, and I can hear everyone groan. ¶ So I've stopped asking questions. It's killing me, but everyone's much more relaxed. They actually like being around me, which should make me feel great; but it doesn't. My questions are eating at me and I'm beginning to wonder if this Jesus stuff is for real. How come no one else has my questions? How come none of my friends are as excited about Jesus as I am? Don't get me wrong...I'm not thinking I'm some cool Christian. I just feel like I'm some kind of freak. Am I? See what I mean? I still can't stop asking questions.

IN THE STORY
Pick one of the questions from the story and answer in as much detail as you can.

May God give you the eyes to see all that you are looking for, the ears to hear what you need to hear, and the patience to receive it in God's time, not yours.

sensitivity

Sensitivity means you're aware of others. You can see what's going on inside, not just outside. You can interpret body language as well as spoken language. A sensitive person looks into other people's eyes and can tell if they're upset, if they're being honest, if they're holding something back, or if they're angry. Sensitive people are observant, but gentle. They don't try to expose others, but rather support them and encourage them—sensitive people know how to truly be with others. Being a Christian doesn't give a person the right to preach to others about their needs or to immediately try to fix those needs. A real disciple notices the need first, works to understand that need, and then decides what to do. Disciples don't exist to fix people, but to notice people.

Mark 5:25-34
Our faith directly affects what we receive from Jesus.

A large crowd followed [Jesus] and pressed around him. And a woman was there who had been subject to bleeding for twelve years. She had suffered a great deal under the care of many doctors and had spent all she had, yet instead of getting better she grew worse. When she heard about Jesus, she came up behind him in the crowd and touched his cloak, because she thought, "If I just touch his clothes, I will be healed." Immediately her bleeding stopped and she felt in her body that she was freed from her suffering.

At once Jesus realized that power had gone out from him. He turned around in the crowd and asked, "Who touched my clothes?"

"You see the people crowding against you," his disciples answered, "and yet you can ask, 'Who touched me?'"

But Jesus kept looking around to see who had done it. Then the woman, knowing what had happened to her, came and fell at his feet and, trembling with fear, told him the whole truth. He said to her, "Daughter, your faith has healed you. Go in peace and be freed from your suffering."

May the God who made the nerve endings on the wing of a fly, make you aware of the little things in the world around you.

Life Hint:
If you build walls around yourself so that no one can ever hurt you,
isn't that the same thing as a prison?

DEVOTI

IN 1990 MC HAMMER RELEASED THE ALBUM *PLEASE HAMMER DON'T HURT 'EM*, WHICH CONTAINED THE SONG "U CAN'T TOUCH THIS" AND BECAME THE NUMBER ONE BEST-SELLING RAP ALBUM IN HISTORY.

FACT FOR THE DAY

TODAY'S TOP 10

MAKE A LIST OF THE TOP TEN THINGS THAT ARE HAPPENING AROUND YOU RIGHT NOW. (BUT THERE'S A CATCH: DON'T LOOK UP FROM THE BOOK.)

JOURNAL ENTRY:

IF I STILL MYSELF, IF I GET REALLY QUIET…THE THING I BECOME MOST AWARE OF IS THE IDEA THAT…

Last night at church my youth worker said, "If you are serious about being a disciple, then you need to care about other people. So why not have lunch with a loner or show attention to someone everyone else ignores?" So I did. ¶ Big mistake. I had lunch with this loner guy, and now he follows me around everywhere I go. There's a reason he's a loner, and now I want him to go back to being a loner. Oh, and get this: I hung around after class to walk this very overweight girl to her next class, trying to be nice to her. Now guess who wants to be my next girlfriend. My friends are having a lot of laughs at my expense. I don't mind helping the needy, but I don't want to be their lifetime buddy.

IN THE STORY

Imagine you are the youth minister who gave this guy the advice. What would you say when he comes to complain?

Someone Just Like You

serv

Servant-like people care for others. True servants actively look for ways to help others by listening, watching, and paying attention. Servants are sensitive. They can tell when someone is hurting or in need. Servants know how to help others so that the one being helped does not feel demeaned or used. Serving is done for the benefit of others, not for the benefit of one's self.

¶ Servanthood is not a one-time experience; it's a way of life—one that takes a lifetime to learn. You don't become Mother Teresa in a

like

week. True servanthood becomes possible as we hang out with Jesus, read about him, think about him, and talk about him. Jesus set the example. He not only washed the disciples' feet; he gave his life for them. ¶ By the way, servanthood is also hard. And humiliating. And awkward. And difficult. But it's also blessed when you do it. Jesus said so.

TODAY'S TOP 10
MAKE A LIST OF THE TOP TEN THINGS YOU'D LIKE TO HAVE SOMEONE ELSE DO FOR YOU.

JOURNAL ENTRY:

IF I HAD NO REASON TO STAY AND EVERY REASON TO GO I WOULD…

John 13:4-5, 12-17

See that guy on his knees washing the grime from between your toes? That's the Son of God.

So he got up from the meal, took off his outer clothing, and wrapped a towel around his waist. After that, he poured water into a basin and began to wash his disciples' feet, drying them with the towel that was wrapped around him. When he had finished washing their feet, he put on his clothes and returned to his place. "Do you understand what I have done for you?" he asked them. "You call me 'Teacher' and 'Lord,' and rightly so, for that is what I am. Now that I, your Lord and Teacher, have washed your feet, you also should wash one another's feet. I have set you an example that you should do as I have done for you. I tell you the truth, no servant is greater than his master, nor is a messenger greater than the one who sent him. Now that you know these things, you will be blessed if you do them."

May the God who is on his knees bring you to yours.

Someone Just Like You

The small-group leader had told Daryl he would really enjoy helping at the Special Olympics this year. Daryl thought: *Oh, what the heck. I've never been around mentally challenged people before. I don't think I've even talked to someone with Down syndrome, so it might be cool.* Daryl showed up for the Special Olympics and was introduced to Ellie, a young high school girl with Down syndrome. Daryl took a liking to her immediately and took it upon himself to be her personal servant all day. Ellie had entered three races: the 50-, 100-, and 200-yard dashes. The first two went okay. Ellie didn't win either of them, but didn't seem to mind. ¶ As the day wore on, Daryl's experience with Ellie became more difficult and tiring. Daryl found it hard to understand Ellie when she talked—and she talked all the time. She became stubborn and uncooperative, even rude. To be honest, Ellie started to irritate Daryl, but he decided he could tough it out for one more hour until Ellie's last race ended. Ellie was very tired and very irritable when the last race was announced. She alternated between refusing to move and crying. Daryl felt helpless and frustrated. He became short with her: "Ellie! Quit being a jerk, and quit whining. You signed up for the race, and you're going to honor your commitment." Ellie reluctantly agreed and did fine until about halfway through the 200-meter race. Suddenly she stopped running. The rest of the runners stopped, grabbed her hand, and tried to get her to run with them. Ellie refused. The rest of the runners finally went on. ¶ Daryl was fed up with Ellie now. He walked over to her on the track and, without thinking, yelled at her, "Ellie, you are really acting selfish. Stop being so uncooperative!"

¶ Ellie looked at him as tears slipped silently down her face. "I'm sworrry, Daryl. I...I...don't feel so gwood." As Daryl turned back to her, she suddenly lunged forward and vomited all over the front of him. ¶ Daryl couldn't believe how disgusting and awful this experience had turned out to be. Obviously angry, Daryl helped Ellie clean up, then he cleaned himself off and left as quickly as he could. He couldn't wait to get home and take a shower. The whole drive home he was thinking: Yeah, servanthood is great. You try to help people who don't want your help, won't cooperate, and then throw up all over you. Fine, I did it once. Never again.

When Daryl got out of the shower his mother was standing at the door with the portable phone. "Phone call, Daryl. Says he is the father of Ellie, whoever that is." *Oh great,* Daryl thought, *now I'm going to get a lecture from him.* Daryl grabbed the phone. "Hello?" ¶ "Hello, Daryl, this is Don Sykes, Ellie's dad. She wants to talk to you." ¶ Before Daryl could react, Ellie was on the phone. She was crying softly. "Uh, Dwaryl, I want to thank you for helping me today. Nobwody ever do that for me. I'm sworry I wasn't bery nice. I didn't feel gwood." Daryl wasn't feeling well himself. "But I guess you know I wasn't fweeling gwood. I thwow up on you." Then she began to cry, "I sworry, Dwaryl." ¶ Daryl was trying to hold back the tears himself. "It's okay, Ellie. I'm sorry for getting so mad at you." ¶ "Oh, it's okay, Dwaryl," Ellie said. "I forgwive you. Lots of people get mad at me, but you didn't get mad like they do. Would...would you be my fwiend?" ¶ Daryl was now very choked up. "Yes, Ellie, I would like to be your friend." ¶

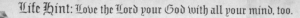

Shrewdness is a word you don't hear used much today. It certainly doesn't sound very Christian, does it? Shrewd has a sneaky, devious, scheming, and shifty sound to it. Yet Jesus suggested that being shrewd is a good thing. What the heck is he talking about? To find out, let's use another term for shrewd: street smart. That's what Jesus is saying. He's suggesting that Christians need to know the neighborhood. They need to know how to navigate their way through a world that is sneaky, devious, scheming, and shifty. People who are street smart aren't evil; they're survivors. They know the safe places to go and the dangerous places to avoid. They know how to survive! ¶ Think about how many times Jesus asked the Pharisees questions he knew they couldn't answer publicly. Jesus continually set up the Pharisees so they couldn't answer Jesus without getting in trouble with the crowds. He was shrewd. Being a disciple is not only about following Jesus; it's also about using your mind, keeping your eyes open, and being tough when you need to be. Being shrewd means following Jesus with your heart and your street smarts.

Luke 16:1-9
Parable of the Shrewd Manager.

FACT FOR THE DAY

A SHREW IS A MOUSE-LIKE CREATURE THAT UNTIL RECENTLY WAS THOUGHT TO BE THE WORLD'S SMALLEST MAMMAL. (SOME BARELY MEASURING AN INCH IN LENGTH). THEY HELD GREAT SIGNIFICANCE IN ANCIENT EGYPT AND WERE OFTEN MUMMIFIED WITH THE PHARAOHS TO REPRESENT THE "DARK" SIDE OF LIFE WHERE A MONGOOSE WAS REPRESENTATIVE OF THE "LIGHT."

SOURCE: HTTP://MEMBERS.VIENNA.AT/SHREW/INDEX.HTML

Jesus told his disciples: "There was a rich man whose manager was accused of wasting his possessions. So he called him in and asked him, 'What is this I hear about you? Give an account of your management, because you cannot be manager any longer.'

"The manager said to himself, 'What shall I do now? My master is taking away my job. I'm not strong enough to dig, and I'm ashamed to beg—I know what I'll do so that, when I lose my job here, people will welcome me into their houses.'

"So he called in each one of his master's debtors. He asked the first, 'How much do you owe my master?'

"'Eight hundred gallons of olive oil,' he replied.

"The manager told him, 'Take your bill, sit down quickly, and make it four hundred.'

"Then he asked the second, 'And how much do you owe?'

"'A thousand bushels of wheat,' he replied.

"He told him, 'Take your bill and make it eight hundred.'

"The master commended the dishonest manager because he had acted shrewdly. For the people of this world are more shrewd in dealing with their own kind than are the people of the light. I tell you, use worldly wealth to gain friends for yourselves, so that when it is gone, you will be welcomed into eternal dwellings.

May God give you that special kind of wisdom that makes you wise beyond your years and wise beyond the wisdom of those who think they are smarter than you.

Someone Just Like You

Danielle was angry. In all her years as a Christian she couldn't remember being so mad. She wasn't angry with a friend or family member, though. She was angry with her church. The congregation had decided to spend three million dollars to build a new "Family Life Center." The Center was advertised as a great way to evangelize the neighborhood by providing a "safe, pleasant atmosphere for families to be together." Danielle may have been only 16, but she knew what the phrase meant. It meant the church people didn't want to use public facilities for racquetball, swimming, and working out. It meant the church people didn't want to be "contaminated" by non-Christians. ¶ Danielle had complained to her parents, her youth minister, and her pastor to no avail. "Three million dollars could go a long way in Haiti or Africa or any one of a hundred different missions," she protested. All she received in return was a pat on the head and words like "That's a wonderful idea, Danielle, but our church already gives to missions." ¶ So Danielle came up with a plan that she didn't share with any adults. She simply spread the word to all the kids in the youth group. The plan was to call the kids, have them show up at the annual business meeting where the congregation was going to vote on the Family Life Center, and issue a challenge to the church. The challenge was simple: "We, the young people, challenge the congregation to match the money spent on the Family Life Center and use it for world hunger." Danielle had it all planned. During the vote, all the young people would stand, walk to the front of the fellowship hall, and announce their proposal. ¶ First Church was a large congregation, and more than 300 young people showed up, each with a poster that read "Our families live while other families are dying." Danielle called the newspaper and a local TV station to tell them of her plan. What a meeting! Danielle spoke for all the young people and said, in front of the cameras and microphones, "We're not against the Family Life Center, but we are against our families living while other families are dying. We are willing to give up our entire youth budget so that families around the world can live. All we're asking is that for every one dollar the church spends on the Family Life Center, it matches that dollar by spending it on world hunger." ¶ It took only about a minute before someone in the congregation suggested the church match every dollar spent on the Center with a dollar spent on world hunger. Two years later, the church has its Family Life Center and has raised three million dollars for hunger relief around the world.

JOURNAL ENTRY:

IMAGINE YOU HAVE A GROUP OF FRIENDS
WHO DON'T LIKE TO TALK ABOUT GOD
AND YOU HAVE SOMETHING REALLY GREAT
TO SAY...BUT YOU KNOW THAT THEY'LL ALL
JUST LOOK AT YOU SO...

Strength means stable, durable, impregnable, rugged, passionate, intense, and constant. Admit it: there are moments, days, weeks, even months when you feel strong, passionate, and zealous. That's good. During our strong moments we feel invincible, impregnable, and powerful—like nothing can defeat us or get us down. When we feel strong, there's nothing like it. It's a "mountaintop moment" when no one can cause us to weaken or stumble. ¶ Yet no matter how strong we feel, weakness is always just a moment away. Read the passage below again. Notice that Peter is the strong one. Yet he's just a few months away from being the weak one. Feeling strong can trick us into believing we will never be weak. Good disciples understand that strength never stays with us, so we must always be prepared for the weakness that is as much a part of being a disciple as strength is. We must always remember that our strength is not in our feelings, but in Jesus who is our strength even when we feel weak (1 Corinthians 1:25).

John 6:60, 60-69
It's hard. Deal with it.

On hearing [Jesus' words], many of his disciples said, "This is a hard teaching. Who can accept it?"

Aware that his disciples were grumbling about this, Jesus said to them, "Does this offend you? What if you see the Son of Man ascend to where he was before! The Spirit gives life; the flesh counts for nothing. The words I have spoken to you are spirit and they are life. Yet there are some of you who do not believe." For Jesus had known from the beginning which of them did not believe and who would betray him. He went on to say, "This is why I told you that no one can come to me unless the Father has enabled him." From this time many of his disciples turned back and no longer followed him.

"You do not want to leave too, do you?" Jesus asked the Twelve.

Simon Peter answered him, "Lord, to whom shall we go? You have the words of eternal life. We believe and know that you are the Holy One of God."

Life Hint:
Jesus never promised to solve your problems for you. He did, however, promise to stay beside you and give you strength to face them yourself.

May God give you strength and all the necessary wisdom and patience to go with it.

TODAY'S **TOP 10**

MAKE A LIST OF THE TOP TEN STRONG
PEOPLE YOU KNOW PERSONALLY.
(DON'T COUNT PHYSICAL STRENGTH.)

JOURNAL ENTRY:

IF I GO TO THE GYM AND WORK OUT
EVERY DAY, I CAN GET STRONG…PHYSICALLY. I
WANT TO BE SPIRITUALLY STRONG, SO I
NEED…

FACT FOR THE DAY

THE STRONGEST CREATURE ON THE
PLANET IS THE RHINOCEROS BEETLE.
AN AFRICAN ELEPHANT CAN CARRY
UP TO 25 TIMES ITS OWN WEIGHT. A
RHINOCEROS BEETLE CAN CARRY UP
TO 850 TIMES ITS OWN WEIGHT.* *SOURCE:
WWW.EXTREMESCIENCE.COM

IN THE STORY

Imagine Logan gets an e-mail from a friend who asks,
"How are you feeling?" Write Logan's response.

strength

Someone Just Like You

Logan was blown away. She had never experienced the nearness of God like she had at camp. She'd never been able to stand in front of a group of kids and say anything, even at school. Not only was she shy, but also crowds made her very nervous. But there she was, standing in front of 50 kids, telling them about Jesus and what he meant to her. What's weird is that she wasn't afraid, and with every word she felt stronger and bolder. Watching her friends stare at her in amazement gave her even more confidence. ¶ There was no doubt in Logan's mind that this Jesus stuff was real. It had changed her life, and she wanted everyone to know about it. Earlier in the evening, she had called her parents to tell them she was going to stand up at campfire and tell the kids about her relationship with Jesus. She could tell her parents were pleasantly shocked. She could hear it in their voices. They kept asking her if she was all right. She thought to herself, *All right? I'm more right than I've ever been.* She went to sleep that night feeling like a new person, just like the Bible said.   ¶ However, a week after camp, Logan found her old fears coming back. She had decided to talk about her faith in Christ as part of a report for English class on her goals in life. The night before the report was due, Logan felt very afraid. *I can't do this,* she thought. *Everyone will think I'm crazy. Maybe I am. I can't talk about Jesus in front of my English class. Come on, God, where are you? Help me to be strong. I can do this, and I know you can help me.* ¶ The next morning Logan woke up feeling nauseated and weak. When she threw up her dinner from the night before, Logan's parents decided she'd better stay home. She felt relieved until the guilt hit her: *Great, Logan, you really are a strong Christian, all right. You can't even keep your dinner down. Face it, you were just all emotional at camp, that's all. Now it's back to the real world.*

JOURNAL ENTRY:

I GET THE WHOLE "THEY ARE WEAK BUT HE IS STRONG" THING, BUT I STILL WANT TO KNOW WHY...

TODAY'S TOP 10

MAKE A LIST OF THE TOP TEN THINGS ON YOUR MIND THAT YOU'RE READY TO GIVE TO GOD.

Kristin didn't want to get out of bed. Her entire body ached. She was sick to her stomach, and it seemed as though every part of her was in pain. How could last night have happened? Kristin had never been more miserable. She felt embarrassed, humiliated, angry, disgusted, guilty, hurt, and disappointed. ¶ Kristin had been going to Bible study every week. She woke up every morning one hour early to pray and read her Bible. Not only was she in an organized small group that met once a week, she had recently begun meeting in a special accountability group with Cheryl and Grace. The members of the group were supposed to keep each other accountable and ask for support when they were in trouble. But Kristin doubted that she would ever be able to admit what had happened. ¶ It was finals week, and Kristin had been studying late every night. She figured she'd slept about eight hours total for the whole week. The night after her last final she decided to celebrate with her boyfriend, Kenny. They were going to a movie and then to Veggies, a new restaurant for vegetarians, for a late-night snack. Just as she and Kenny were leaving her house, Kristin's mom called. "I . . . uh . . . have to work late, Kristin. Don't wait up for me." ¶ Kristin knew what her mom meant. Her mom had been married three times and seemed to have a new boyfriend every other week. She usually ended up sleeping with her boyfriends and sneaking in at about four in the morning. Kristin's mother was a pathetic example of a parent. ¶ Kristin could feel the anger inside. "Fine, Mom, whatever," she said and hung up. She was so angry she said to Kenny, "Let's just go to your place and rent a video. I don't feel like going out." ¶ Kenny agreed very enthusiastically. "Sure. My folks are gone for a couple of days, anyway." ¶ Kristin normally would have said no, but tonight she just didn't care. No parents, no sleep, no mom, and one beer, and the next thing Kristin knew, she and Kenny were undressed and very close to having sex. Somehow she was able to pull herself away, grab her clothes, and run out of the house; but she had violated every Christian value she had. Some disciple she was.

IN THE STORY

You are Kristin's best friend. She just called you and told you everything that just happened. What's the first thing out of your mouth?

Matthew 26:36-41
You're getting verrry sleeeepy...

Then Jesus went with his disciples to a place called Gethsemane, and he said to them, "Sit here while I go over there and pray." He took Peter and the two sons of Zebedee along with him, and he began to be sorrowful and troubled. Then he said to them, "My soul is overwhelmed with sorrow to the point of death. Stay here and keep watch with me."

Going a little farther, he fell with his face to the ground and prayed, "My Father, if it is possible, may this cup be taken from me. Yet not as I will, but as you will." Then he returned to his disciples and found them sleeping. "Could you men not keep watch with me for one hour?" he asked Peter. "Watch and pray so that you will not fall into temptation. The spirit is willing, but the body is weak."

WEAKNESS.

Weak may be a very negative-sounding word, but it describes an unfortunate truth: human beings are not strong. Whether we're Christians or non-Christians, young or old, healthy or sick, weakness is a fact of life. That's important to understand because there are different kinds of weakness: weakness caused by disease, weakness caused by emotional problems, and weakness caused by not taking care of one's self. Then there are our natural weaknesses: we have to eat; we have to exercise; we have to drink liquids; and we have to sleep. No matter how dedicated a Christian you are, you have to eat, drink, exercise, and sleep. ¶ It's important that we understand our weaknesses and not deny them. The limitations of our bodies have an effect on the rest of our lives. If we are deprived of sleep, drink, exercise, or food, we are susceptible to illness, irritation, bad judgment, and faulty thinking. In other words, we find ourselves making dumb mistakes and bad decisions. ¶ Disciples have bodily needs. If we don't take care of our human weaknesses, then we end up missing opportunities we wish we hadn't missed. The disciples who fell asleep didn't sin, but they did miss out on helping their Lord at a critical time. Imagine how many times after Jesus died those disciples wished they could have relived that night.

May the God of strength and awesome power surround you in your weakest moments. May he send his guiding angels to come and stand around your chair.